The Pathological Vision:
Jean Genet, Louis-Ferdinand Céline, and Tennessee Williams

American University Studies

Series III
Comparative Literature

Vol. 5

PETER LANG
New York · Frankfort on the Main · Berne

Robert Hauptman

The Pathological Vision

Jean Genet, Louis-Ferdinand Céline, and Tennessee Williams

PETER LANG
New York · Frankfort on the Main · Berne

CIP-Kurztitelaufnahme der Deutschen Bibliothek

Hauptman, Robert:
The pathological vision: Jean Genet, Louis-
Ferdinand Céline, and Tennessee Williams /
Robert Hauptman. – New York; Berne; Frankfort
on the Main: Lang, 1983.
    (American university studies: Ser. 3,
    Comparative literature; Vol. 5)
    ISBN 0-8204-0037-8

NE: American university studies / 03

Library of Congress Card Number: 83-48747
ISBN: 0-8204-0037-8
ISSN 0724-1445

© Peter Lang Publishing Inc., New York 1984

Printed by Lang Druck Inc., Liebefeld/Berne (Switzerland)

"Es un desierto circular el mundo,
el cielo está cerrado y el infierno vacío."

--Octavio Paz

"Only through mastering unmitigated
evil does existence attain to transfiguration."

--Martin   Buber

Contents

Preface

The three essays included in this study are concerned with a particular ontological perspective. One can indicate that an author is pessimistic or optimistic; analogously, his ontology may be seen as normal or pathological. It is the contention of these essays that the microcosms created by Genet, Céline, and Williams reflect an aberrant, pathological ontology.

It is no surprise that critics refer to these writers in terms of a unified Weltanschauung.[1] A vision, a world, demands totality; the critic who insists upon unity but nonetheless discusses the Weltanschauung in terms of its components, that is, the separate books, is doing the author a disservice. It is for that reason that each of these "visionaries" will be treated thematically. Since a total vision is not definable from the perspective of a single work, each of these essays encompasses a body of writings. Genet is viewed from the perspective of his five prose pieces; Céline's vision is derived from the four major novels; Williams is discussed in terms of ten major plays.

The following abbreviations are used to indicate primary sources:
Jean Genet

    LADY--OUR LADY OF THE FLOWERS

    MIRACLE--MIRACLE OF THE ROSE

    FUNERAL--FUNERAL RITES

    JOURNAL--THE THIEF'S JOURNAL

    QUERELLE--QUERELLE OF BREST

Louis-Ferdinand Céline:

    JOURNEY--JOURNEY TO THE END OF THE NIGHT

DEATH--DEATH ON THE INSTALLMENT PLAN

GUIGNOL--GUIGNOL'S BAND

CASTLE--CASTLE TO CASTLE

Tennessee Williams

STREETCAR--A STREETCAR NAMED DESIRE

BABY--BABY DOLL

CAMINO--CAMINO REAL

CAT--CAT ON A HOT TIN ROOF

MENAGERIE--THE GLASS MENAGERIE

MILK TRAIN--THE MILK TRAIN DOESN'T STOP HERE ANYMORE

IGUANA--THE NIGHT OF THE IGUANA

TATTOO--THE ROSE TATTOO

SUDDENLY--SUDDENLY LAST SUMMER

BIRD--SWEET BIRD OF YOUTH

Finally, I take this opportunity to acknowledge my sincere appreciation to all those who contributed to the completion of this study. I am especially grateful to Terry Hauptman for her understanding, to Dr. Arvin Wells for his time, helpful suggestions, and encouragement, and to Sarah Morrison for her editorial assistence.

1. JEAN GENET: EVIL APOTHEOSIZED

Un phare ironique, infernal,
Flambeau des grâces sataniques,
Soulagement et gloires uniques,
--La conscience dans le Mal!

--Charles Baudelaire

The term "pathological action" must of necessity remain ambiguous. Innumerable factors are involved in classifying an action, and if any of of those varies, the action can no longer be considered pathological. Given the wide range of opinions, even within disciplines such as psychology, sociology, philosophy, and literature, it would be surprising indeed if a consensus could be reached. Most commentators on pathological action stress, however, that rigidity of response is indicative of a diseased perspective. Thus Kubie feels that

> The essence of normality [health] is flexibility.... The essence of illness is the freezing of behavior into unalterable and insatiable patterns. It is this which characterizes every manifestation of psychopathology, whether in impulse, purpose, act, thought, or feeling.[1]

He further insists that compulsive repetition implies neurosis:

> Any moment of behavior is neurotic <u>if the process that set it in motion predetermines its automatic repetition</u>, and this irrespective of the situation or the social or personal values or consequences of the act.[2]

Kubie might be termed a "situational behaviorist." As Joseph Fletcher believes that all ethical action depends on the particular circumstances, so Kubie feels that all action is indeterminant. A static response is untenable. For Kubie cultural norms, as well as frequency of action, ethical considerations, and legal knowledge, are not valid criteria. Kubie, like Freud, refuses to acknowledge the seminal role that cultural patterns ultimately play in a determination of pathological action. That is strange given Horney's post-Freudian clarification of neurosis. Whereas Freud could make anthropological observations and unabashedly extrapolate a theory about man in general (see TOTEM AND TABOO), Horney believes that cultural patterns must not be ignored:

> There are two characteristics, however, which one may discern in all neuroses without having an intimate knowledge of the personality structure: a certain rigidity in reaction and a discrepancy between potentialities and accomplishments.... Rigidity, however, is indicative of a neurosis only when it deviates from the cultural patterns.[3]

If we accept that, lack of stability is also a characteristic of neurotic individuals along with rigidity of response and deviation from cultural norms, we have a working definition of pathological action. Glover is more definite:

> The true psychopath ... exhibits a general instability of emotion, thought and conduct, is frequently sexually perverted and often anti-social: in fact the psychopath was formerly described as a "moral imbecile."[4]

With few exceptions the characters who inhabit Genet's, Céline's, and Williams's microcosms manifest emotional instability, rigidity of response, and deviation from cultural norms. The picture that emerges from the interplay of their characters is distinctly pathological. To these writers, human beings are psychically wounded creatures who sully everything with which they come into contact. Whether the characters are clinically or socially aberrant makes little difference.[5] In the final analysis men and women become dismal parodies of themselves.

Genet's world can be aptly described in terms of a system of ever-increasing concentric circles. As unstructured, desultory, and ramifying as the novels are, they nonetheless adhere ontologically, axiologically, and ethically to a set of a priori axioms that constitute a stringently closed system comparable, paradoxically, to Dante's

Christological order. The system is complex, mystifying, and all-inclusive. It too has its theocracy, angels, dogma, values, rewards and punishments.

Thody describes the Genet microcosm as a "consistent if heretical world view,"[6] although he then unaccountably goes on to contradict himself by indicting Genet for "his total inability to cast his ideas into a consistent world view"[7] The validity of the latter supposition is, however, highly questionable. Yeager is far less equivocal. He compares Genet's order to the catechism in Christianity: "Genet's work offers us, once his initial postulates are accepted, an equally closed system in which all experience is accounted for."[8]

At the center of the cosmos is Jean Genet, hereafter referred to as Jean, the overt or covert protagonist in all but one of the prose works and the implicit narrator in the final novel, QUERELLE OF BREST. His is a Jeanocentric universe. All being revolves around him; all being ramifies from him, is a reflection of him, and ultimately returns to him. Coe chooses the mirror as the metaphor to describe this vision. Esslin in his discussion of absurd drama does the same; yet a mirror's nature allows it only to reflect what is presented to it, even though it may aggrandize, distort, contort, or otherwise alter reality. A reader is thus forced to put on the garb of the metaphysician, at least momentarily, and peek behind or underneath the metaphorical mirror. Why is Jean, this ramifying reflector, the center of the vision? Answering that question will help readers and critics alike to understand the significance of the mirror metaphor and ultimately to concretize Genet's vision.

Jean is a narcissist, a narcissist with solipsistic tendencies. The literal world will continue if he ceases to exist; yet he is the measure of all being. If he loves only himself and himself in those he loves, and if all other lovers are merely manifestations of himself, he is concomitantly capable of despising himself and all others. Hatred or self-hatred is for Jean a form of self-aggrandizement. He remains Narcissus.

Offer and Sabshin note that "the neurotic man is self-centered and without a social conscience."[9] If such egocentricity is carried to its logical conclusion, the result will be unmitigated narcissism. For Freud the conclusion is simply the totally gratifying experience of treating one's body as a sexual object. There are several reasons for this "object choice," and Freud lists four.
One loves,

1. What one is oneself (that is oneself)
2. What one once was
3. What one would like to be
4. Someone who was once part of oneself[10]

Genet, as Sartre points out, worships himself; he sees himself everywhere. Thus Jean is egocentric, egomaniacal, narcissistic. When he chooses to become the center of the universe, he predicates an absolute attitude towards himself. Not only do he and those who are a manifestation of him love in terms of the Freudian quadrad, but Jean also amplifies and embellishes the possibilities so that they become infinite. Jean loves his actual self. He speaks of the "pleasure of the solitary, gesture of solitude that makes you sufficient unto yourself" (LADY, p. 129). On perceiving a multiplicty of Jeans, he says, "When I tell one of them that I love him, I wonder whether I am not telling it to myself" (LADY, p. 257). He also loves what he becomes under the influence of another, that is, through an act of conjoining: "The lads I speak of evaporate. All that remains of them is what remains of me: I exist only through them who are nothing, existing only through me" (JOURNAL, p. 94). He states, [Friendship's fire] would, I thought, turn against me, who contain and detain Jean's image and allow it to merge with myself within me" (FUNERAL, p. 28). If he is frustrated in an attempt to assimilate another's being, he may shift perspectives. Thus, when sexual love is precluded through the death of Jean Decarnin (because necrophilia at this point appears unacceptable, though it does occur in another context) Jean becomes anthropophagous. What he would like to be, in this manner can literally be assimilated into his system: "I could have carried his body.... I could have cut it up in a kitchen and eaten it" (FUNERAL, p. 32). If all physical contact must cease, a mental transposition suffices and is accepted as fact: "Jean himself inhabits me.... He is inside me" (FUNERAL, pp. 98, 99). Ultimately the confusion is total. Jean can no longer differentiate between the external sexual object and his physical or metaphorical assimilation of it. Through this process of coalescence he is free to substitute one for the other: "I shall publish it [FUNERAL RITES] so that it may serve Jean's glory, but which Jean?" (FUNERAL, p. 164).

Jean idealizes both past and future. What he once was is loved in terms of what he believes himself to have been. At Mettray he loves a fellow colonist, named Divers, whom he resembles, but since there are no mirrors available, he remains only partially conscious of this. Years later at Fontevrault, he again encounters Divers, and although this "mysterious resemblance" is partially imaginary, it nonetheless serves to heighten a rebirth of love. As Jean poignantly puts it,

> He finally believed in my love for him. After fifteen years of waiting, of seeking--for since his departure from Mettray, my entire life, as I now realize, had been only a long quest for him--I had risked death to see him again. (MIRACLE, p. 128)

A more complex form of narcissitic behavior is the coalescence of Jean with other characters, for example, with Culafroy, who becomes Divine; or consider Jean, the implicit narrator of QUERELLE, who ultimately becomes Querelle, not merely because the murderer is a projection of himself but also because of Jean's adulation and envy. Coalescence reaches epic proportions in OUR LADY when Jean euologizes the murderer:

To love a murderer.

I am tired of satisfying my desire for murder stealthily by admiring the imperial pomp of sunsets. My eyes have bathed in them enough. Let's get to my hands. But to kill, to kill you, Jean. Wouldn't it be a question of knowing how I would behave as I watched you die by my hand? (LADY, p. 120)

It is not mere sophistry to derive the following syllogism:

1. Jean loves the murderer.
2. He murders himself.
3. He therefore loves himself, as murderer and victim simultaneously.

Thus the love of self is the basis for the dual nature of Genet's world. Because self is a reflection of self, all things become reflections of their twins, and then in true solipsistic fashion return to the final source, Jean. There is, however, an additional complication. In Genet's vision the source of all being is not externalized. Heaven, Hell, and God are all centrally located in Jean's cerebrum, viscera, or bowels. This is not the Augustinian metaphorically internalized God, nor even the Hindu avatar. This is the omnipotent creator, Jean--homosexual, thief, traitor, and fantasizer.

Thus, the Jeanocentric universe turns out to be theocentric as well, although Jean is an erratic and peculiar god. First, he is not as powerful nor as omniscient as he sometimes would have the reader believe. Second, he is a grotesque distortion of the normal depiction of a benevolent or vindictive creator. Jean manifests various attitudes toward such a God. Frequently, the deity is pictured in prosaic terms, and at times Jean equivocates between himself and the palliating being who might succor him. Of greatest significance, nonetheless, is Jean himself. In THE THIEF'S JOURNAL he offers the etiology of his apotheosis:

> Much solitude has forced me to become my own companion. Envisaging the external world, its indefiniteness, its confusion, which is even more perfect at night, I set it up as a divinity of which I was not only the cherished pretext, an object of great care and caution, chosen and led in masterly fashion, though through painful and exhausting ordeals, to the verge of despair, but also the sole object of all this labor. And little by little, through a kind of operation which I cannot quite describe, without modifying the dimensions of my body, and perhaps because it was easier to contain so precious a reason for such glory, it was within me that I established this divinity--origin and disposition of myself. I swallowed it. (JOURNAL, pp. 85--86)

This assimilation leads to the impression "that the idea of God is something I harbor in my bowels" (JOURNAL, p. 173). The attempt to hypostatize the deity is a conscious and concerted one: "My goal is God. I am aiming at Him" (FUNERAL, p. 199); "I was sure that I was the god. I was God" (FUNERAL, p. 248); and finally," On Judgement Day it will be with my own voice that God will call me: Jean, Jean!" (LADY, p. 246).

As God is a creator, so too is Jean. He is ostensibly responsible for the prose narratives being related and directly responsible for the fantasies that spring from them, as well as for the new axiological perspective posited. Ex nihilo nihil fit. Hence Jean begins with basic premises, concepts, or actualities, and he transvalues, remolds, and otherwise rearticulates the universe in his own terms. His metaphysic is really quite simple. The world is bifurcate: paradoxical as it may appear, given the complex structure articulated, a veritable, palpable physical world can be differentiated from the secondary imaginary, at times phantasmagorical realm. These two worlds intermingle, interact, and influence each other in the most convoluted fashion, though Jean and those whom he discusses (for example, Divine, Darling, Querelle, and Seblon) usually remain conscious of them as separate entities. In their minds the two realms do not merge into one nebulous quagmire. Reality is not amorphous. It only appears to be.

Time is amorphous, and for that reason it causes Genet's fiction to appear unstructured and desultory when it really is not. Genet's spatial-temporal beginning is invariably an actual present (the moment of literary conception) within the physical world. Thence follows a reversion to the actual physical past. Then, as Jean meanders through the halls of Fontevrault, the streets of Paris, or the enigmas of metaphysics, he subtly shifts into an imaginary realm of dream, fantasy, and hallucination that exists in both of the temporal spheres. In its most extreme form--for example, in FUNERAL RITES--the characters of actuality who are secondarily transposed into a visionary reality create a tertiary reality of their own. This tertiary reality in turn ramifies back to Jean's physical world, namely, to the demise of his young lover, Jean Decarnin. The different realms may be represented graphically:

```
                         REALM OF THE                    REALM  OF  THE
PHYSICAL ——————present—— PRIMARY        ——————present ———— SECONDARY
REALM    ——————past    —— IMAGINATION   ——————past     —— IMAGINATION
```

A particular temporal sphere can result in either a present or a past in the subsequent realm. A physical present leading to an imaginary present would be hallucinatory in nature; a physical present leading to an imaginary past would, however, be oneiric.

Jean sufers from "Camus's disease," a nostalgic longing for meaningfulness that continually encounters an unresponsive external universe. Jean will internalize meaningful experience (a process analogous to Camus's "philosophical suicide") rather than accept the consequences of absurdity. Thus Coe's emphasis on the void and nothingness in Genét seems to be misplaced. Unlike Beckett or Ionesco, Genet creates an extremely viable, if grotesque, metaphysic, aesthetic, and axiology--in fact, a total Weltanschauung--despite his occasional negations: "This book [is a] ... pursuit of the impossible nothingness" (JOURNAL, p. 94).

The imaginary realm's encroachment upon the actual stems from Jean's longing for meaningfulness. Because Jean is escaping into the imaginary realm (usually remaining, however, conscious of its disparity with physical reality), he may at times be guilty of intentional self-delusion. For example, when opting for abjection as salvation, he craves the life of a transported convict. Since transportation of convicts is no longer the government policy, he says: "But I am speaking of a penal colony which has been abolished. Let me therefore restore it in secret and live there in spirit, as in spirit Christians suffer the passion" (JOURNAL, p. 256). The imaginary realm allows for the subjugation of the actual.

The nostalgic need to create meaningfulness and to negate hardship moves the narrative into a third sphere, the idealized physical, about which Jean is explicit if contradictory: "The boredom of my prison days made me take refuge in my past life, even though it was vagrant, austere, or destitute" (JOURNAL, p. 109). Of course, this destitution, the life of a colonist at Mettray reformatory, becomes glorified, sacred in Jean's mind. On the other hand, as colonists Jean and his cohorts also idealize the future. It is their fondest desire to be worthy of Fontevrault prison, in the shadow of which Mettray is situated. Thus from a particular physical perspective the past is recalled, or the future is augured, in idealized terms. Later Jean insists that the beauty that he saw in prison life generally is no longer there. The ideal is destroyed: "I no longer hoped that prison would remain what it had long been, a fabulous world.... I saw prison as any ordinary roughneck sees it" (MIRACLE, p. 25). His psychological motives are far more complex than the explanation that he provides, which is, as he puts it, that his childhood is dead. Whether Jean likes, dislikes, likes because he dislikes, or pretends to like for an ulterior motive depends on the particular situation.

If the idealized physical is not utilized, then the very act of imaginative creation mitigates for Jean the squalor of prison life:

> Yet, back in my 426, the sweetness of my work entrances me. The first steps I take, with my hands on my hips, which seem to be pitching, makes me feel as if Darling, who is walking behind, were passing through me. And here I am again in the soothing comfort of the elegant hotel which they will have to leave, for twenty thousand francs is not eternal. (LADY, p. 132)

Jean becomes Darling. A mental and physical (kinesthetic) transformation occurs, as it does when Jean infuses himself into the being of other characters. This transformation is insidiously expressed through an indistinct shift in personal pronouns:

> For a few days Culafroy was also one of them. He fed on crusts, covered with hair, that he found in garbage cans. One night, the night he was most hungry, he even wanted to kill himself. Suicide was his great preoccupation: the song of phenobarbital! Certain attacks brought him so close to death that I wonder how he escaped it, what imperceptible shock--coming from whom?--pushed him back from the brink. But one day there would be, within arm's reach, a phial of poison, and I would have only to put it to my mouth; and then to wait. (LADY, p. 94)

> Motionless at the center of a state of perfect lucidity--so extradorinary that he [Erik] feared for a moment lest the purity of his vision radiate outside him and illuminate Riton--he let the kid alone and was amused by his playing. I withdrew my finger and very skillfully succeeded in undoing two buttons. This time I put my whole hand in. I squeezed, and Erik recognized, I don't know how, that I was squeezing tenderly. He didn't stir. (FUNERAL, p. 156)

The incursion of the imaginary may become a conscious game. Then it is most closely related to a dream state. Consider Divine, the male become female through illusion and appearance: dress, gesture, and speech result in a new reality that Divine foists on herself, her cronies, and the unsuspecting stranger. Within this first game a second develops. Neglected by her lovers, "with her head beneath the sheets, she would devise complicated debauches, involving two, three, or four person." But, "the pleasure soon lost its edge. Divine then donned the body of a male" and finally "sought out the memory of Alberto and satisfied herself with him" (LADY, pp. 156, 157). Thus, the fantasy or dream satisfies a physiopsychological need. The people who inhabit Genet's universe are fantasizers; they recreate reality in their own terms: "These games were carried on consciously, not for the purpose of deceiving, but of enchanting" (LADY, p. 201). The most extended dream-image is the galley that Jean periodically discusses. It too serves to alleviate the distress of the moment by presenting the mind with an enticing fantasy. In this "otherworldly universe" that Jean inhabits,

> Mettray suddenly takes the place--not of the prison in which I live, but of myself--and I embark, as formerly deep in my hammock, on the remains of the half-destroyed unmasted ship among the flowers of the Big Square at Mettray. My longing for flight and love disguises her as a mutinous galley that has escaped from a penal colony. She is the "Offensive." I have roamed the South Seas on her through the branches, leaves, flowers, and birds of Touraine. (MIRACLE, p. 89)

The individual dream images that make up the entire galley sequence are interpolated directly into the text, at times with little or no transition:

> When I dreamed of a prick, it was always Harcamone's--which was invisible at the Colony--in his white canvas trousers. Now, that prick, as I learned later from one of those indiscretions common among hoodlums, did not exist. The prick merged with Harcamone; never smiling, he was himself the stern organ of a

> supernaturally strong and handsome male. It took me a long time to know of whom. The truth of the matter is that Harcamone belonged to a pirate prince who had heard about us. From his galley, among his coppery riffraff, that is, also covered with copper ornaments, sailing and sizzling far from here, he had sent us his superb organ, which was as ill-concealed in the guise of a young mason as the murderer himself would have been in the guise of a rose.
> (MIRACLE, p. 206)

Within the imaginary realm a further leap is made, and Harcamone becomes a pirate's organ sent to Mettray, ostensibly as a gift. The apex of the dream-imagination is the desire to be outstanding (egregious) not in actuality but internally: "my longing for a splendid imaginary destiny" results in the creation of "Weidmann, Pilorge, Socaly--in my desire to be them" (LADY, p. 256).

In MIRACLE OF THE ROSE, Jean, "the disenchanted visionary," experiences the ultimate epiphany, Harcamone's apotheosis. This is the miracle toward which the narrative is directed. Its early manifestations are posited christologically so that the final experience is easily seen in religious-mystical terms:

> Harcamone "appeared unto me".... I felt in all my veins that the miracle was under way. But the fervor of our admiration and the burden of saintliness which weighed on the chain that gripped his wrists--his hair had had time to grow and the curls had matted over his forehead with the cunning cruelty of the twists of the crown of thorns--caused the chain to be transformed before our scarcely astonished eyes into a garland of white flowers. The transformation began at the left wrist, which it encircled with a bracelet of flowers, and continued along the chain, from link to link, to the right wrist. Harcamone kept walking, heedless of the prodigy. The guards saw nothing abnormal. (MIRACLE, pp. 15-16)

This is merely a preview, but it serves to illustrate the hallucinatory aspect of Jean's imaginative leaps. The ineffable quality of the experience is evident in the guards' demeanor. The novel depicts Harcamone slowly winding his way down the road to apotheosis: "Finally on the fortieth night, I had a revelation: Harcamone's cell appeared within me" (MIRACLE, p. 319). The miracle is described as follows:

> He approached the door, holding up his irons, but hardly had he taken three or four steps when the irons opened and fell to the floor noiselessly. Harcamone did not fluster. He must have been used to the courtesy of objects. He pressed his ear to the door and listened: the guard was asleep. He filled his lungs with air. The thing was going to be difficult. He therefore uttered a silent invocation: he summoned all his energy. Magical operations are exhausting. They drain you. A person cannot perform them twice in one day. You must therefore succeed at the first try. He went through. (MIRACLE, p. 323)

It is followed by an ascension:

> Without growing an inch, he became huge, overtopping and splitting the cell, filling the universe, and the four black men shrank until they were no bigger than four bedbugs. The reader has realized that Harcamone was invested with such majesty and that his clothes themselves were ennobled and turned to silk and brocade. (MIRACLE, p. 334)

The four shrunken men then invade Harcamone's interior and discover the "Mystic Rose" at the center of his heart. This sequence of hallucinations impinges on Jean's perception of reality, but it differs from what I term the dream-image because it is externalized while the dream-image remains pure internal fantasy. Dreams are perceived with the mind's eye; hallucinations, on the other hand, appear to be physically palpable.

With the exception of FUNERAL RITES the structures of Genet's major prose works are quite simple. The foregoing discussion has made that clear. Once the spatio-temporal shifts are understood, there are few problems to contend with. That, however, is not entirely true of FUNERAL RITES. As indicated above, the physical and imaginary realms tend to blend together in amorphous time in Genet's works. Although the various realms, it should be reiterated, are usually distinguishable, the interconvolutions are indeed complex. Figure 1 shows the different spheres of reality in FUNERAL RITES.

Fig. 1. Physical and Imaginary Realms in Jean Genet's FUNERAL RITES

I. Physical Present	II. Imaginary Past	III. Secondary Imaginary Past and Present
Mother and Erik	Erik and Berlin executioner	Riton ("kills" Jean)
Jean D., Paulo	Jean G.	_____ and Erik
Maid, Jean G.	Paulo and Jean G. as Hitler	_____ and Paulo _____ and German soldiers

A selection of the more blatant transpositions will suffice to indicate both the complexity and the pathological nature of the fantasies. During a film Jean sees a young traitor on the screen:

> My hatred of the militiaman was so intense, so beautiful, that it was equivalent to the strongest love. No doubt it was he who had killed Jean. I desired him. I was suffering so because of Jean's death that I was willing to do anything to forget about him. The best trick I could play on that fierce gang known as destiny, which delegates a kid to do its work, and the best I could play on the kid, would be to invest him with the love I felt for his victim. I implored the little fellow's image: "I'd like you to have killed him!" (FUNERAL, pp. 54-55)

For Jean this is exactly what happens. Illusion becomes reality, and Jean Decarnin is "killed" by Riton, the traitor. What is important in this context is that the fantasy is extended and encroaches on both reality and other fantasies. Ultimately the illusion becomes more significant than actuality. In conjunction with these secondary fantasies occur the less complex self-identifications of Jean with Hitler:

> Gerard, who was the master of my secret revels, had the right to enter immediately when I was alone. He therefore entered,

pushing in front of him a pale, young French hoodlum with a cap
in his hand. The boy was not particularly surprised at finding
himself in the presence of the most powerful man of the age.
Hitler stood up, for he knew that the politeness of kings is
exquisite, and put out his hand to Paulo, whose amazement and
horror began that very moment. (FUNERAL, p. 127)

Driver indicates that here Genet (that is, Jean) "appropriated the misery of
millions to his own psychological needs."[11] This is an anticipatory
indication of the pathological nature of his fantasizing. A similar
transposition occurs during a casual meeting with Erik:

I loved Erik. I love him. And as I lay in the Louis XV bed,
Jean's soul enveloped the bedroom in which the naked Erik was
operating with hard precision. I turned away from Paulo. With
my head in the hollow of his legs, my eyes sought the sacred
crabs, and then my tongue, which tried to touch that precise and
tiny point: a single one of them. My tongue grew sharper,
pushed aside the hairs very delicately, and finally, in the
bushes, I had the joy of feeling beneath my papillae the slight
relief of a crablet. At first, I dared not remove my tongue. I
stayed there, careful to keep the joy of my discovery at the top
of my tongue and of myself. (FUNERAL, p. 243)

There is, of course, no basis for the love other than a momentary
fascination "opened by disgust." Paulo, Jean's mental lover in the Hitlerian
scenes, is peremptorily discarded. Additionally, and this will be elaborated
upon below, Jean manifests his love in a rather grotesque manner.

A brief comment on the pathology of dream, fantasy, and hallucination
is in order here. The encroachment of illusion upon reality, resulting in a
new suprareality, is the keystone of Genet's vision. The ambiguous
ontological perspective that Jean creates allows him total freedom of action.
It does not, however, imply that an axiological or ethical response is not
expected of the reader. Jean himself is conscious of the unreasonable
aspect of his creations: "I made the same movement that religious fanatics
make to seize the hem of a cloak and kiss it" (MIRACLE, p. 16). The
fanatic is a man who wears solidly attached blinders and therefore can see
only a predetermined goal.

This study is not meant to be psychoanalytical in nature, and the typical Freudian paraphernalia--oral, anal, and Oedipal--is stringently avoided. Yet Freud is generally helpful when he abstains from theorizing and simply indicates his observations:

> From pathology we have come to know a large number of states in which the boundary line between ego and outer world becomes uncertain, or in which they are actually incorrectly perceived--cases in which parts of a man's own body, even component parts of his own mind, perceptions, thoughts, feelings, appear to him alien and not belonging to himself; other cases in which a man ascribes to the external world things that clearly originate in himself, and that ought to be acknowledged by him. So the ego's cognizance of itself is subject to disturbance, and the boundaries between it and the outer world are not immovable. [12]

Even more germane are the similarities between the fantasies of sociosexual misfits and neurotics or even psychotics:

> The well-known fancies of perverts which under favorable conditions may be changed into actions, the delusional fears of paranoiacs which are in a hostile manner projected on others, and the unconscious fancies of hysterics which are discovered in their symptoms by psychoanalysis, agree as to content in the minutest details. [13]

The connections between the dreams of Genet's characters and the various kinds of pathological dreams are not the only indications we have that his characters are not socially viable. If Genet's fantasizers are viewed from a humanistic-psychological perspective, the resulting picture is equally damning. Van Kaam believes that "people who live a life of neurotic fantasy often reveal that they cherish dreams of momentous events which are to happen to them."[14] Further he says that those who inhabit "a twilight of fantasy and dream ... live a counterfeit life."[15] Questions relating to the relative authenticity of experience are complex and perhaps can never be resolved, though much has been said on the subject. Maurice Friedman is especially clear in TO DENY OUR NOTHINGNESS, but to enter at this point into a discussion concerning authentic action would simply obfuscate the problem at hand. Suffice it to say that Jean, Divine, Darling, Seblon, Querelle, and the others are guilty of counterfeiting existence. This comment is not meant as a condemnation of visionaries such as Baudelaire, Rimbaud, and Van Gogh. Only those who become dependent on the fantasy are culpable. Rimbaud's persona is reacting authentically, affirming his responsibility within the human condition, when he says at the conclusion of "A Season in Hell"

> Moi! moi qui me suis dit mage ou ange,
> dispensé de toute morale, je suis rendu
> au sol, avec un devoir à chercher, et la
> réalité rugueuse à étreindre! Paysan!

Even though he is rather unhappy about it. "It is very rare," observes Malraux, "for a man to be able to endure ... his condition, his fate as a man." The fantasies created in Genet's world are mere palliatives that allow his characters to evade rather than affirm their condition, their fate.

The emphasis in Genet study is frequently placed on the metaphysical or symbolic, perhaps to the detriment of our understanding of the works (see, for example, Coe or Gerber). Here it is the axiological and ethical that are deemed most significant. Genet begins with the social norm, revalues it in terms of his perception of evil, and purposively creates a new moral order, a new value systems. This process, shown graphically in Figure 2, is not arbitrary, but rather an a priori necessity for survival. Van Kaam affirms man's axiological heritage:

> Our motivational life has grown from a matrix of values which we
> have in common with mankind as it has developed within the
> Western Tradition. In other words, our personal existence is

Figure 2.   Genet's Transvaluation of Social Norms

Norm = moral order   Norm Transvalued = new moral order
                                                  in   terms   of   evil

Superannuated Norm

axiological, ethical spheres

---

embedded in a larger existence which is that of Western man. The values and motivations common to the Western world are realized, to be sure, in different degrees in various personalities.[16]

Yet what happens when this "matrix of values" becomes superannuated? Glicksberg observes: "The tragic pessimism of modern literature is born of the knowledge that the universe conforms to no moral order and exemplifies no pattern of divine justice."[17] When the universal ethic breaks down, the moral order that man has derived from it is no longer viable. All men do not necessarily founder in an adiaphorous bog, but some certainly do. For Ionesco or Beckett the resulting sense of absurdity leads to a philosophical void. At this very point, however, facing the abyss of nothingness or adiaphorous response, Genet makes a leap of faith and affirmation by recreating not only reality but also its values. Genet, like Baudelaire, affirms, albeit in a negative fashion. This is the very antithesis of absolute negation:

Et mon coeur s'effraya d'envier maint pauvre homme
Courant avec ferveuer à l'abime béant,
Et qui, soûl de son sang, préférerait en somme
La douleur à la mort et l'enfer au néant!

Baudelaire and Beckett are antipodes.

The transvaluation does not imply that the accepted moral order is absolutely untenable, and certainly Genet does not expect universal acceptance of his transvalued norms. His particular order cannot be extrapolated beyond his system. Such an extrapolation would defeat its purpose, which is to achieve total solitude. Jean posits in various ways his attempt to create the new order. Articulation occurs not

> because I wanted to relive my emotions or to communicate them, but rather because I hoped, by expressing them in a form that they themselves imposed, to construct an order (a moral order) that was unknown (above all to me too). (JOURNAL, pp. 171-72)

As the new order takes shape, Jean is more specific:

> A morality is being born, which is certainly not the usual morality (it is consonant with Divine) though it is a morality all the same, with its Good and Evil. (LADY, p. 99)

Ultimately this becomes "an ethic contrary to the one which governs the world" (JOURNAL, p. 182). An ethic of "moral solitude":

> It was by raising to the level of virtue, for my own use, the opposite of the common virtues that I thought I could attain a moral solitude where I would never be joined. I chose to be a traitor, thief, informer, hater, destroyer, despiser, coward. With ax and cries I cut the bonds that held me to the world of customary morality. (FUNERAL, pp. 170-71)

The revaluation allows Jean to stand beyond the pale of society and outside much of the criminal world that he inhabits. He becomes a law unto himself. Thus he is not beyond good and evil but simply in another axiological realm. There is excellent Nietzschean precedent for this, and Nietzsche himself is far more convincing when he affirms transvaluation than when he speaks of the nebulous realm beyond good and evil:

> For all the value that the true, the truthful, the selfless may deserve, it would still be possible that a higher and more fundamental value for life might have to be ascribed to deception,

> selfishness, and lust. It might even be possible that what constitutes the value of these good and revered things is precisely that they are insidiously related, tied to, and involved with these wicked, seemingly opposite things--maybe even one with them in essence.[18]

Here Nietzsche is hardly negating value; he is simply restructuring it. And this is continually Jean's perspective as well. Occasionally amoral activity is implied, but it is after all amoral only in relation to a societal norm. After Village murders Sonia,

> By a powerful effort of will, he escaped banality--maintaining his mind in a superhuman region, where he was a god, creating at one stroke a private universe where his acts escaped moral control. (LADY, p. 176)

Secondly, amorality is peremptorily negated as a possibility:

> For Divine, to commit a crime in order to free oneself from the yoke of the moral powers is still to be tied up with the moral. (LADY, p. 295)

Genet's cosmos is highly structured both axiologically (because the new values are continually alluded to) and ethically (because the "correct" form of action is discussed and depicted). Thus Gerber's opinion that the imaginary realms allow for an adiaphorous response is nonsense: "By relating as dream-content certain actions which are odious to accepted social mores, Genet wishes to bring about an abeyance of the reader's moral judgment of these events, since dream is a state of the unconscious and relieves its agent of moral responsibility."[19] These "odious actions" are performed within a prescribed "moral order" and are often actual events rather than fantasies. They demand a moral response. Barish is far less equivocal; rather than rationalizing Genet's method, he simply observes what is achieved. Speaking specifically of OUR LADY OF THE FLOWERS, he says: "The vilest, most literally nauseating phenomena are transvalued into fulgurations of beauty and evidence of sainthood. The whole traditional vocabulary of mysticism is used to transfigure the most revolting squalors."[20] Genet uses this method throughout his prose works, and the reader is forced to accept the transvalued ethic in its own terms, disquieting as it may be.

Moralists generally avoid defining the good, much less the summum bonum. Yet in a social context the good is easily discerned. It is toward its antipode that Jean and his fellow characters gravitate. Evil is sought, and for the "purest" of those who inhabit Genet's world, it is sought as an absolute. In this sense evil becomes their good. The transvaluing process takes that logical direction. Thody, however, disagrees:

> Genet ... has no concept of goodness and no desire to achieve it. He is aiming at absolute evil, and the inclusion of any rational argument, of any search for pleasure, would introduce positive qualities into what must remain an entirely negative world.[21]

He fails to realize that Genet's characters ascribe all of the properties of good to evil. That does not mean that good and evil are necessarily synonymous but rather that the social evil becomes a new good. Consequently, the social good becomes the new evil, that which is to be avoided. For this reason even Coe, who is certainly more accurate in his analysis, is rather misleading:

> All Genet's novels are concerned with a search for the Absolute--whether for an Absolute Good or an Absolute Evil is, in the long run, essentially indifferent, and indeed, in those ultimate domains of thought, beyond time and space, to which he eventually leads us, the one becomes indistinguishable from the other.[22]

That this is not entirely accurate is obvious:

> But if I display such passion in discarding good, it's because I'm passionately attached to it. And if evil arouses such passion, it's because it itself is a good, since one can love only what is good, that is, alive. (FUNERAL, p. 213)

Joad observes "Nobody does what is evil for its own sake. He only does evil as a means to something else which he takes to be good."[23] For Jean, consequently, absolute evil as an end in itself is a simulacrum. It is actually a means to numerous other ends, for example, the solitude of the outsider, the pleasure taken (perverse though it may be) in subjugation, abjection, various forms of destruction, love in all of its guises, and ultimately sainthood. The epitome of social goodness is Jean's goal, though sainthood in Genet's world is obviously invested with grotesque attributes, including as it does all of the characteristics that constitute the new axio-ethical system. This antipodal canonization should come as no surprise. The final step in the transvaluation process would logically be the creation of the sacred. If Ricoeur can say that "evil is supremely the crucial experience of the sacred,"[24] then Genet's revaluation is almost defensible from a normative perspective, for, as Schopenhauer notes, "evil is just what is positive; it makes its own existence felt." If it is true that evil is sanctified within an axiological framework, as the foregoing allege, it is astonishing that critics refuse to acknowlege Genet as a creator of values. Instead they assert, "The fact is that Genet's position, in moral terms, is a wholly nihilistic one," and "he has no belief in any structure of values.[25] These statements appear to be misinterpretations at the very least.

Genet's axio-ethical orientation, that is, the transvaluation of social norms in terms of evil, is patholgical for several reasons. We have observed that Jean-become-God is the center around which the world revolves. This is repeated in metaphorical terms: as God, Jean is the source of value and ethical action. The new perspective must, however, be distorted. As van Kaam says, "Self-centeredness, the refusal to be man and not God, is the core of the demonic in human nature."[26] When men attempt to encompass the absolute as an extension of their own wills, they assuredly affirm evil, and, psychologically speaking, theirs is a pathological response. Transvaluation conforms to the pattern of neurotic behavior described above. A certain perverse rigidity of response occurs in the revaluations, as well as blatant deviations from social norms. At the same time the behavior manifested is detrimental to the inhabitants of these spheres, both "normal" men and transvaluers. Finally, there is an interesting ethical note: Jean's actions do not conform to the Kantian dictum that one's actions be universalized with no detrimental effect. In fact, that is the antithesis of what Jean desires, since it would destroy his deistic position, his solitude, and his saintliness. For example, when Jean stumbles through Nazi Germany, he discovers that evil is no longer enticing:

> "It's a race of thieves," I thought to myself. "If I steal here, I perform no singular deed that might fulfill me. I obey the customary order; I do not destroy it. I am not committing evil. I am not upsetting anything. The outragious is impossible. I'm stealing in the void." (JOURNAL, p. 123)

Genet's axio-ethical realm can be divided into four primary sections: the hierarchy of power, crime, love and its ramifications, and sainthood. Each of these will be discussed separately. In order, however, fully to appreciate what Genet achieves, it is necessary to mention two factors. First, Genet employs the incongruous image, a common poetic device, that in his work frequently takes the form of an analogy. The most flagrant of these images are Christological and thus heighten the distaste that Genet aims to create. Secondly, to Jean these images are potent, since he does indeed perceive the world in religious terms, and the discrepancy between the analogues results in an esoteric beauty.

"Un soir," says Rimbaud, "J'ai assis la Beauté sur mes genoux.--Et je l'ai trouvée amère.--Et je l'ai injuriée." Conversely, degradation, evil and ugliness, become beautiful in Genet's universe. Whereas Rimbaud finds beauty distasteful, Genet recreates it in his own image. Hence he says that "the beauty of a moral act depends on the beauty of its expression" (JOURNAL, p. 22). Beauty is the progenitor of good and evil and since Genet affirms the evil, it becomes his good. The aesthetic merit of this evil then becomes the criterion by which its ethical viability is judged. Beauty is fleeting and requires cruelty (MIRACLE, pp. 8, 246); ultimately it is derived from an intuitive feeling:

> Though they [moralists] may prove to me that an act is detestable because of the harm it does, only I can decide, and that by the song it evokes within me, as to its beauty and elegance; only I can reject or accept it. (JOURNAL, pp. 192-93)

This is a vicious circle, since it is axiomatic that evil or crime (murder, betrayal, theft) is invariably beautiful, whereas sacrifice, humility, or charity is invariably ugly. Obviously the former will evoke internal nightingales, hence elegance and beauty: "I recognize in thieves, traitors and murderers, in the ruthless and the cunning, a deep beauty--a sunken beauty--which I deny you" (JOURNAL, p. 111). Beauty becomes by inversion ugliness.

The hierarchy of power is extremely important in the world that Genet depicts. The allocation of power (social, physical, intellectual, and imaginary) to some, and the allocation of impotence to others, is, of course, the basis upon which societies are structured. Within society, however, there usually is a gradual extension of power and the fervent desire to partake of power is limited. In Genet's world the characters are always part of a blatant power structure that is for the most part distinct rather than progressive; a gamut of power does not exist within any given context. Instead there are once again distinct antitheses which are expressed grapically in Figure 3.

Figure 3. Power in Society Versus Power in Genet's World

	Weakest	Weaker	Strong	Stronger	Strongest
Society					
Genet's World	Weak				Strong

In discussing THE MAIDS, Coe alleges that "in a social context ... power is pure appearance."[27] One is powerful only because one seems to be. In fact, this spurious form of power plays only a minimal role in Genet's world, where those who are termed powerful can back up their claims.

The role that Jean plays within the hierarchy of power varies from novel to novel. At times he stands outside the hierarchy and simply determines the status of other characters but that stance is only temporary. In both OUR LADY OF THE FLOWERS and QUERELLE OF BREST, for example, he eventually becomes assimilated into the characters of Divine and Querelle respectively. Nietzsche, in a rather Darwinian fashion, defends the structure of power: "life itself is essentially appropriation, injury, overpowering of what is alien and weaker; suppression, hardness, imposition of one's own forms, incorporation and at least, at its mildest exploitation."[28] In this sense power is ineluctably palpable, hardly mere appearance.

The most blatant display of structuring occurs in MIRACLE OF THE ROSE, where a remarkable pecking order is established in each of the social spheres. The young hooligans at Mettray fall into three classes: big shots, chickens, and jerks. Despite the extensive terminology and subtle distinctions that Genet employs, nothing really intervenes between the toughs and their chickens. The big shots are the source of power and are respected and feared. At times, it is true, the younger big shots may become chickens in relation to the older big shots, but that appears to be an infrequent occurrence. In the homosexual relationships the big shots play the male role to their chickens, whom they own and protect. The jerks are nonentities, totally dehumanized creatures who are apparently unworthy of inclusion in the system at all. Interestingly enough, the inhabitants of the colony do not acknowlege the power of "the external world." They do not, for example, respect the power of the wardenship, because it exists outside the world that they create for themselves.

The marriage that occurs between a tough and his chicken solidifies not only the relationship of the two individuals but also the tradition of usurpation of the weak by the strong: "I belonged to him [Divers] from the very first day" (MIRACLE, p. 81). This reification of man is the mildest form of dehumanization or exploitation in Genet's world. Consider the simultaneous assault by Villeroy (Jean's big shot) and Jean on a young boy, who consequently becomes Jean's chicken. Although Mettray is largely divided into two opposing camps, namely, the weak and the strong, Jean also notes a sexual hierarchy:

> I was still astounded at the thought that each male had his own glorious male, that the world of force and manly beauty loved in that way within itself, from link to link, forming a garland of muscular and twisted or stiff and thorny flowers. Those pimps were always being woman for someone stronger and handsomer than they. They were women less and less the further away they were from me, all the way to the very pure pimp who dominated them all, the one who lorded it over the galley, whose lovely penis, grave and distant, moved about the Colony in the form of a mason. Harcamone! (MIRACLE, p. 262)

Fontevrault prison is structured in a similar fashion. In fact, many of the Mettray big shots and chickens meet there again years later and pick up where they left off. Here the nomenclature used to designate convicts is derived from their social professions: queen, crasher, pimp, murderer. Yet the hierarchy remains much the same: the dominant toughs versus the weaklings. In both spheres the power of the strong is frequently affirmed in a physical manner. Death is therefore a common occurrence.

The ethic of power holds sway outside of prison as well, with some variations. Querelle, the proud, strong murderer, becomes the dominant figure in a complex setup where sexual domination takes precedence over social importance. The basic pattern is evident in the social domination of Querelle by his lieutenant, Seblon, and by his antithesis, the detective Mario. Yet Querelle in turn dominates Seblon sexually, since the lieutenant harbors a fond desire to sleep with him. Mario too is socially superior, but ultimately fails to assert this prerogative. Nono is dominant sexually, but Querelle chooses to accept from him this form of abjection, which is concomitantly an indication of power. Of course, Querelle controls the destinies of Gil, Vic, and his other victims. This is the most basic pattern of domination; the further complications of Querelle's twin brother and Madame Lysiane do not amplify the question at hand.

One final point that must be mentioned is the belief shared by Genet's characters that power is transmissible, that the dominant person can initiate the fledgeling into a cult of power that he in turn will carry on after maturation. The characters in FUNERAL RITES consistently exhibit this behavior. For exmaple, Erik is the naive catamite of the Berlin executioner, a man with absolute power over his victims. Some of this power is infused into Erik, who then continues the chain by becoming the pederast in a new relationship with Riton, who in turns "kills" Jean Decarnin. Analagously, Jean-as-Hitler, "the master of the world," begins the process again with Paulo. "The power of the Reich" can thus be transmitted in an exorbitant sexual fashion. Finally, the ethic of power comes full circle: "Thus, acts have esthetic and moral value only insofar as those who perform them are endowed with power" (LADY, p. 171), and "the regime of force [is the] protector of Beauty" (LADY, p. 213).

In general, the evil that Jean seeks is manifested in the form of crime, of which there are three primary types: theft, betrayal, and murder. The evil of crime becomes the stepping-stone to the solitude that will ultimately be synonymous with sainthood. Hence criminal acts take on a mystical, emotional significance totally incommensurate with what they achieve. They are freqently unprofitable and even foolhardy, yet Jean, Darling, and Querelle feel illuminated by them. The hypostatization of a new ethic thus gives rise to an aesthetic response. Horney alleges that such responses indicate patholgocial behavior and, much of what follows must be seen in the light of her lucid analysis:

> In the striving for possession hostility usually takes the form of a tendency to deprive others. The wish to cheat, steal from, exploit or frustrate others is not in itself neurotic. It may be culturally patterned, or it may be warranted by the actual situation, or it may normally be considered a question of expediency. In the neurotic person, however, these tendencies are highly charged with emotion. Even if the positive advantages he derives from them are slight or irrelevant he will feel elated and triumphant if he meets with success.[29]

In fact, Genet's characters exceed the limits outlined above and invest the criminal act with a numinous quality, which is perhaps proportionate to the heinousness of the crime. It is in these terms that Jean describes a theft:

> The theft I had committed became in my eyes a very hard, very pure, almost luminous act, which only the diamond can symbolize.

I had, in achieving it, destroyed once again--and, I thought to myself, once and for all--the dear bonds of brotherhood. (Journal, p. 81)

The "moral perfection" and subsequent solitude achieved is the precursor of sainthood.

Another incident that points up the pathological nature of theft in Genet's novels is Darling's compulsive shoplifting. He has little control over his actions. Since this is frequently true of other characters also, it is not difficult to understand why they all tend toward recidivism. They are not simply existentially hypostatizing an inner tendency as Sartre insists, but compulsively acting out an insuperable need:

He was at the mercy of the will of "another," who stuffed his pockets with objects which, when he got to his room and put them on the table, he did not recognize, for the sign which made him choose them at the moement of theft was hardly common to the Divinity and Darling. (LADY, p. 243)

To protect himself, Darling at times utilizes the following ruse:

He had, on several occasions, already engaged in the following game: on a showcase, among the objects on display and in the most inaccesible spot, he would place, as if inadvertently, some trifling object that had been bought and duly paid for at a distant counter. He would let it lie there for a few minutes, ignoring its existence, and examine the surrounding displays. When the object had melted sufficiently into the rest of the display, he would steal it. Twice a store detective had caught him, and twice the management had been obliged to excuse itself, since darling had the sales' slip. (LADY, p. 244)

Treason is rather more opprobrious and therefore the more favored misdeed. In conjunction with theft it is an excellent source of edification, as is depicted in the following dialogue, where Java's perfidy is incomprehensible to the thief, René:

René asked me whether I knew any queers he could rob. "Not your pals, naturally. Your pals are out." I thought for a few minutes and finally hit upon Pierre W., at whose home Java had stayed for a few days. Pierre W., an old queer (of fifty), bald,

and affected, who wore steel-rimmed glasses. Java, who had met
him on the Riviera, said to me: "He puts them on the dresser
when he makes love." One day, just for the fun of it, I asked
him whether he was fond of Pierre W.
"You love him, admit it."
"You're crazy. I don't love him. But he's a good pal."
"Do you admire him?"
"Well, yes. He fed me. He even sent me some dough."
He had told me this six months before.
I asked him:
"Isn't there anything to swipe at Pierre's?"
"Not much, you know. He's got a gold watch."
"Is that all?"
"He may have some money, but you'd have to look for it."
René wanted exact details. He got them from Java who even
agreed to make an appointment with his former lover and lead him
into a trap where René would rob him. When he left us, René
said to me: "Java's pretty lousy. You've got to be a real heel
to do what he's doing. You know, I wouldn't dare." (JOURNAL,
pp. 246-47)

Jean affirms his love in analogous terms: "I feared and loved him too much

not to want to deceive and betray and rob him" (JOURNAL, p. 261). This

is exactly what he does to another friend, whose money should have been

mailed to jail:

The money was there, intact. I left and tore up the bills,
meaning to throw them into a sewer, but, the better to provoke
the break, I pasted them together on a bench and then treated
myself to a sumptuous lunch. Pépé must have been dying of
hunger in jail, but I thought that by means of this crime I had
freed myself of moral preoccupations. (JOURNAL, p. 79)

Betrayal is pure crime; it allows the traitor to fulfill and "transcend"

himself; as one of Genet's characters insists, "I longed to betray"

(FUNERAL, p. 181). It is the attempt to affirm absolute evil.

It is murder, however, that is lauded most dazzlingly in Genet's

novels. OUR LADY OF THE FLOWERS is a panegyric to Weidmann, Angel

Sun, Maurice Pilorge, and a young ensign, three of whom are murderers.

In order to depict the development of this ontology of destruction, it is

necessary to look at six separate murders. Each is perpetrated for a

different reason and each seems to lead logically to the next: Our Lady kills for remuneration, Daniel for revenge, Divine for substitution, Erik for discovery, Riton for love, and Querelle for no reason at all.

Our Lady, at the tender age of sixteen, kills an old man in order to steal his money. In doing so, he feels that he is fulfilling his destiny in mystical terms and metamorphosing into Our Lady of the Flowers. Yet this is clearly a rationalization, because he subsequently tears through the old man's apartment searching for his reward: "Where does the bastard keep his dough?" (LADY, p. 118). Thus, although a preconceived mystical attitude exists, it is not as significant in this case as it will be in the less materialistic, spiritual murders.

To kill because of unmitigated hatred is not unusual, but in the case of Daniel, the punishment is hardly commensurate with the crime. Sister Zoé simply hits him and then dismisses him from the infirmary at Mettray. He retaliates soon afterwards by shoving her into the pond, where she silently drowns. After that,

> The child, with another jerk of his shoulder, readjusted the red and white sling of his bugle, put his hands back into his pockets and calmly and slowly walked away from the pond. (MIRACLE, p. 285)

Daniel so dehumanizes the sister that he no longer thinks of her as a person, and his extraordinary callousness thus becomes comprehensible. Both of these murders occur in the material sphere, although the reward is minimal, and the murderers feel no regret. The four murders that follow occur in the metaphysical sphere, and Horney's analysis becomes more applicable as the progression develops.

Divine's murder is based on two needs: her impending canonization and a desire to destroy herself. Instead she chooses to substitute a child, whose destruction leads her to sainthood:

> One of her neighbors had a two-year-old baby girl to whom
> Divine used to give candy and who occasionally came to visit her.
> The child would run to the balcony and look at the street
> through the netting. One day, Divine made up her mind: she
> detached the netting and left it leaning against the railing. When
> the little girl came to see her, she locked her in and ran
> downstairs. When she got to the yard, she waited for the child
> to go and play on the balcony and lean against the railing. The
> weight of her body made her fall into the void. (LADY, p. 297)

She destroys both herself and her goodness by killing another. Therefore she is canonized. This is the simplest form of spiritual murder, since, although there is no hope for material gain, Divine nonetheless uses the child's death to satisfy her desires.

Erik, on the other hand, uses much the same terminology, but wishes only to experience the ultimate act of destruction: "I realized that the moment had come to know murder" (FUNERAL, p. 105). He says further: "The highest moment of freedom was attained: to fire on God, to wound him and make him a deadly enemy. I fired. I fired three shots" (FUNERAL, p. 107). The numinous quality ascribed to the murder of this child is peremptorily dismissed by a ludicrous analogy: "I immediately looked at the gun and knew I was truly a murderer, with the muzzle of my revolver like that of the gangsters, the killers, in the comic books of my childhood" (FUNERAL, p. 107-108).

After Erik and Riton consummate their love, Riton mumbles, "I now have the impression that I love you more than before," and then he picks up his machine gun and shoots Erik:

> For ten seconds, a joyous madness was mistress of Riton. For
> ten seconds, he stamped on his friends's corpse. Motionless,
> with his back against the chimney and his eyes staring, he saw
> himself dancing, screaming, jumping about the body and on it and
> crushing it beneath his hobnailed heels. Then he quietly came to
> his senses and slowly made his way to other rooftops.
> (FUNERAL, p. 255)

What I have referred to as spiritual murder, as opposed to material murder, culminates in Querelle's liaison with Vic. Querelle's motives are complex and ambiguous even to himself. All three crimes are involved: theft, betrayal, and murder. Vic, an accomplice in theft, is betrayed and murdered by Querelle--a repetition of similar deeds perpetrated by Querelle in the past. There is no actual necessity for the murder; the comments concerning jewels are mere rationalization. This is an aesthetic deed committed to fulfill an inner emotional need; it is not, as Coe alleges, an existential choice. Coe claims that Genet's murderers place like Sartre "the whole weight of l'être upon the anguished elusiveness of le néant.... This is their gloire. They are the very prophets of Existentialism."[30] Coe further compounds his impassioned pseudophilosophical defense of Querelle by stating, "Whether we find Genet's vision acceptable or not is beside the point."[31] Our response to the act is, however, of primary concern, and the reader's judgment is ultimately based on the metaphysics of the situation, which Coe uses to defend Genet rather than to discover more about him. The reason for an action may not make it acceptable, but it can mitigate its heinousness.

"Killing a man," says Jean, "is the symbol of evil. Killing without anything's compensating for that loss of life is Evil, absolute Evil" (FUNERAL, p. 222). In attempting to achieve absolute evil (that is, sainthood), Querelle is described as an unmitigated psychopath, as the following pasticcio indicates. The "sacred rite" of murder demands the sign of the cross and then

> Querelle felt the presence of death throughout his whole body, the presence of a murderer. He let the stirrings of this emotion ... develop inside him....

> No ... particle of Querelle remain[ed] within his body. His
> body was an empty shell. Facing Vic was no one; the murderer
> was about to attain his perfection. (QUERELLE, pp. 68, 69)

Querelle, like Darling the shoplifter, is a shell, an automaton reacting compulsively not for gain but because he must. All of the pathological characteristics are present: rigidity of response (he has murdered at least three other victims), deviation from the social norm, and especially an emotional exhilaration incommensurate with the achievement--the "rapture that always came to him after committing a crime" (QUERELLE, p. 154). Even the narrator acknowledges "the extraordinary malformations in our hero's soul and body" (QUERELLE, p. 78). The desire to perpetrate evil, to be one's own hagiographer, does not preclude a pathological perspective. Genet tells us, "To escape from horror, as we have said, bury yourself in it" (LADY, p. 119). This is exactly what his characters do. Yet there is indeed a difference between Jean or Querelle and the typical materialistic criminal, a difference pellucidly summed up by Jean (Riton):

> I have killed, pillaged, stolen, betrayed. What glory I've
> attained! But let no run-of-the-mill murderer, thief, or traitor
> take advantage of my reasons. I have gone to too great pains to
> win them. They are valid only for me. That justification cannot
> be used by every Tom, Dick and Harry. I don't like people who
> have no conscience. (FUNERAL, p. 157)

Love and sex, in Genet's world, are analogues. The phrase "I love" is frequently articulated when "I desire physically" is meant. It is unpleasant but nevertheless true that the pathetic creatures who inhabit Genet's universe are abolutely incapable of love. They all live in a dehumanized sphere where only experience is possible, never true relationships. There are explicit reasons for this misinterpretation of love. In order fully to understand them, it is necessary to return to Jean's apotheosis. "The man," alleges van Kaam, "who has deified himself ... can never truly encounter others, even on a peripheral level. He is condemned to play his role always and everywhere."[32] As the measure of all being, Jean is incapable of authentic encounters; and concomitantly so are his coevals, both as manifestations of himself and as similar personalities. Since "man becomes himself only through encounter , which is a transcendence of himself,"[33] there is no possibility for authentic being among Genet's people, who do not transcend but rather descend into and through themselves. Their goals are despair, abjection, sexual gratification, and sainthood.

Even more important to an understanding of Jean's inability fully to realize himself and realize himself in relation to others is van Kaam's excellent dictum: "Human relationships rooted in respect are constructive; rooted in need, they are destructive."[34] Jean, Bulkaen, Erik, and others "relate" out of unmitigated necessity. For them respect is a negative quality and holds no significance. Therefore their various and complex relationships are invariably destructive. At the same time it is possible for them to believe, or to imply that they believe, in a "love" that is nonexistent.

At times the characters themselves indicate that they realize the worthlessness of their love, as when the narrator of QUERELLE states, "The idea of love or lust is a natural corollary to the idea of sea and murder" (QUERELLE, p. 8). For the narrator love and lust are indistinguishable, and both are associated with destructive forces. It is the sexual element that Jean emphasizes philosophically: "Thus do I realize that I have sought only situations charged with erotic intentions. That was what, among other things, guided my life" (JOURNAL, p. 84). Yet even the sexual experience is negated, at least philosophically, because

38

physically it recurs with boring consistency: "I love you.... I love.... I love you" is Jean's affirmation of the erotic experience (JOURNAL, P. 148). Because "love" demands betrayal, as has already been pointed out, and, in fact, "betraying means breaking the laws of love" (JOURNAL, p. 149), love is an impossibility: "We love each other without love" (LADY, p. 110).

In Genet's world the sexual experience is multifaceted, and objects, actions, and people normally not considered in an erotic context become sexually significant.   The act is invariably homosexual in nature; in fact, the female plays such a minimal role in Genet's fiction as to be almost nonexistent.   Dream and fantasy enhance gratification.   At one point even a washbasin is imbued with sexual importance: "Darling has 'fallen' in love" with Divine (LADY, pp. 87-88), but the washbasin is in the context an excellent substitute.   Or the sex act may bcome a monstrous orgy as when Our Lady, Divine, and Seck Gorgui indulge one night in a sequence of purely physical actions (LADY, pp. 232-33).   Similarly, Nono and Querelle use each other in the most sordid, distasteful (to them), automatic, and degrading fashion.   They, in fact, fail to enjoy themselves.   Examples could be multiplied ad nauseam.   Love for Genet's characters is a degraded form of sexual activity.

Although violence plays a minimal role in most human sexual encounters, the violent aspect is disproportionately emphasized by Jean and his coevals.   After Our Lady murders the old man, he fantasizes in a rented hotel room:

All by itself the murderer's hand seeks his penis, which is erect. He strokes it through the sheet, gently at first, with the lightness of a fluttering bird, then grips it, squeezes it hard; finally he discharges into the toothless mouth of the strangled old man. He falls asleep. (LADY, pp. 119-20)

For Our Lady, murder, the ultimate violence, is a prelude to erotic intoxication. The two are indissoluably linked. A second excellent example of this bond occurs in FUNERAL RITES:

> When I heard that Jean had gone to a party despite his oath, I put my gun into my pocket and left with the kid. We went down to the Seine. It was dark. There was nobody around. We were near the parapet, under the trees. My arm was around his neck. "My darling." My mouth was on his ear, and my tongue and lips got busy. He shuddered with pleasure. I got a hard-one. I put my right hand into my pocket and very cautiously took out my gun. My anger was softened by my excitement and loosened its hold. The air was mild. The most serene music descended from the sky to the water and from the trees to us.
> I whispered in Jean's ear:
> "You little bitch, you gave yourself, eh?"
> He thought I was using a lover's language, he smiled. My gun was in my hand and was being caressed by the night air. I pressed the muzzle against the kid's hip and said, in an implacable tone:
> "My finger's on the trigger. If you move, you'll drop." He understood. He murmured, facing the river:
> "Jean!"
> "Don't say a word."
> We stood there motionless The water was flowing with such solemnity that one would have thought it had been delegated by the gods to make the slow course of the drama visible. I said:
> "Wait."
> I withdrew the muzzle that was buried in the cloth of the jacket. At no time did I feel that I was preparing a murder. I added softly: "Do as I tell you. Do it or I'll shoot. Here. Now suck."
> I placed the muzzle of my gun on his parted lips, which he brought together.
> "I'm telling you it's loaded. Suck."
> He opened his mouth and I inserted the tip of the weapon it it.
> I whispered in his ear:
> "Go on, suck it, you little bitch."
> His pride hardened him. He was motionless, unperturbed.
> "Well?"
> I heard the click of his teeth on the steel. He was watching the Seine flow by. His whole body must have been waiting for the lighting that would kill us, the hummed love song that would distract me, the eagle that had been instructed to carry off me, the cop, the child, the dog.
> "Suck or I'll shoot."
> I said it in such a tone that he sucked. My body was pressed against his. With my free hand I stroked his behind.
> "That must give you a hard-on since you like that."
> I delicately contrived to slip my hand into his fly, which I opened. I stroked him, I kneaded him. Little by little he got

excited, though not as stiff as I pride myself that I can make someone if I care to.

"Go on, suck it till it shoots."

I tremble with shame at the memory of that moment, for it was I who gave in. I withdrew the muzzle of the gun from that beautifully curved mouth and moved it to Jean's ribs, at heart level. The Seine kept flowing quietly. Above us, the still foliage of the plane trees was animated by the very spirit of tragic expectation. Things around us dropped their defenses.

"You're lucky, you bitch."

He turned his head slightly toward me. His eyes were shining. He was holding back his tears. "You can talk now. You're lucky I don't have the guts to blast your dirty bitchy little mug."

He looked at me for a second, then turned his eyes away.

"Beat it!"

He looked at me again and walked off. I went home with my weapon lowered. Early next morning he knocked at the door of my room. He took advantage of my usual morning torpor to bring about the reconciliation I longed for. (FUNERAL, pp. 121-23.)

This extreme sexual reponse to violence illustrates what Driver terms "Genet's kind of psychosexual pathology."[35] He says further: "Usually ... we regard the violent component of love as its minor part, subordinated to tenderness, affection, and regard for the partner's welfare. Genet inverts this. Violence becomes the essence of the relationship, its major component."[36]

Hatred elicits a similar response. The more a character finds someone to be despicable, the more he loves him. Consider, for example, Jean's love for the hated Riton or Our Lady's love for his judge: "It is so sweet to love that he could not keep from dissolving into a feeling of sweet, trusting tenderness for the judge" (LADY, p. 286). Violence and related emotions (such as hatred and humiliation) play an important role in the erotic situation--which, according to psychological opinion is another indication of pathology, especially when the sexual acts are sadomasochistic:

One finds that people's attitudes to sex are a reflection of the main forces in their consciousness. Sexual activity often gives expression to our strongest and most poignant attitudes or needs. A sex relation is a profound experience, and in undergoing it, other profound emotions and qualities of the individual are activated. This explains how sexual activity in some people can be stirred up by completely nonsexual situations, such as those involving humiliation, triumph, viciousness, or revenge. A deeply destructive person is bound to express and fulfill these tendencies in sexual activity as well as elsewhere. The converse of this is that once a connection has been formed between sex and destructiveness, then a destructive act may become sexually stimulating in and of itself. It is in this way that sexual acts of masochism and sadism arise.[37]

Genet's characters fixate on certain body parts, which become fetishes to them; instead of becoming the means to sexually gratifying ends, the erogenous parts become ends in themselves. This displacement of value is manifested in the deification of the phallus. Freud, in THREE CONTRIBUTIONS TO THE THEORY OF SEX, insists that the genitals cannot be beautiful (an assertion that he repeats in CIVILIZATION AND ITS DISCONTENTS in slightly abridged form):

I have no doubt that the concept of beauty is rooted in the soil of sexual stimulation and signified originally that which is sexually exciting. The more remarkable, therefore, is the fact that the genitals, the sight of which provokes the greatest sexual excitement, can really never be considered "beautiful."[38]

Jean, however, is not convinced:

Of the tangible him [Darling] there remains, sad to say, only the plaster cast that Divine herself made of his cock, which was gigantic when erect. The most impressive thing about it is the vigor, hence the beauty, of that part which goes from the anus to the tip of the penis. (LADY, p. 60)

The adulation that Genet's characters accord to the sexual organs is epitomized (perhaps unconsciously parodied) in one of the most interesting if repulsive aspects of Genet's universe.

Critics shy away from the overt sexuality so rampant in Genet's fiction, euphemistically referring to "erotic" or "pornographic" elements. They do not care to venture into discussion of Genet's coprophilia, which imbues the unpleasant, the offensive, and the repulsive with the aura of beauty. Yet tacitly to disregard this aspect of his oeuvre is to ignore a significant portion of the conscious life of his people. For the purposes of this discussion I divide the human body into three distinct parts: perceptions, functions, and secretions. Under normal circumstances man's senses take precedence over functions and secretions, that is, one is more dependent on and more conscious of sight or hearing than excretion or ejaculation. Jean and company literally ignore their senses; they see, hear, and taste as a matter of course. Touch is a minor exception, for obvious reasons, because without tactility there can be no sexual response. Yet even that sense is taken for granted; it is the response that is emphasized. Smell is the only sense to which homage is rendered:

> I have already spoken of my fondness for odors, the strong odors of the earth, of latrines, of the loins of Arabs and, above all, the odor of my farts, which is not the odor of my shit, a loathsome odor, so much so that here again I bury myself beneath the covers and gather in my cupped hands my crushed farts, which I carry to my nose. They open to me hidden treasures of happiness. (LADY, p. 166)

The importance of bodily functions is also inverted. In descending order of signficance, man depends upon respiration, maintenance of body temperature, drinking, sleeping, ingestion, urination, excretion, and ejaculation. The first five of these are ignored by Genet. Sleeping is important in connection with dreams or fantasies, never for its own sake. Ingestion is mentioned only a few times, usually in connection with a meaningful gesture or an extraneous event such as betrayal, abjection, or punishment. Soup is far less important to Jean after many days in special confinement than his vision of Harcamone. Yet these characters obviously ingest, digest, and assimilate because they excrete and urinate in phenomenal quantities. And they derive once again an incommensurate pleasure from these rather inconsequential procedures. The unpleasantness of this emphasis is heightened by the incongruity of religious imagery:

> Though the matter was not serious, the three years that he spent in the penitentiary were poisoned by the preoccupation with those Sunday mornings--which I now see decorated with garlands of little shirts flowered with light touches of yellow shit, before mass--with the result that on Saturday evenings he would rub the corner of his shirt on the whitewash of the wall to try to whiten it. (LADY, p. 248)

It is superfluous to multiply examples. The following description of Jean-as-Hitler making love to Paulo will suffice:

> It was a rough-and-tumble--or rather a systematic labor--in which I tried in every possible way to return to the larval form by virtue of which one goes back to limbo. Paulo's behind was just a bit hairy. The hairs were blond and curly. I stuck my tongue in and burrowed as far as I could. I was enraptured with the foul smell. My moustache brought back, to my tongue's delight, a little of the muck that sweat and shit formed among Paulo's blond curls. I poked about with my snout, I got stuck in the muck, I even bit--I wanted to tear the muscles of the orifice to shreds and get all the way in, like the rat in the famous torture, like the rats in the Paris sewers which devoured my finest soldiers. (FUNERAL, p. 139)

Bodily secretions are inordinately important: mucous, saliva, tears, blood, dandruff, urine, feces, gas, and semen. Parasitic creatures, such as lice and crabs, are also relevant in this context. Bodily secretions become criteria for judgment: "The shit amassed in Jean's intestine, his slow, heavy blood, his sperm, his tears, his mud, were not your shit, your blood, your sperm" (FUNERAL p. 62). Two final examples illustrate the grotesqueries associated with secretions and parasites:

> I do not remember whether I had lice. In any case, I have never devoured any. My head was covered with dandruff that formed a crust which I would scrape off with my nail and then knock from my nail with my teeth, and which I sometimes swallowed. (LADY, p. 300)

> A few of the crabs he had probably picked up from a whore still clung to me. I was sure that the insects had lived on his body,

if not all of them at least one whose brood invaded my bush with
a colony that was digging in, multiplying, and dying in the folds
of the skin of my balls. I saw to it that they stayed there and in
the vicinity. It pleased me to think that they retained a dim
memory of that same place on Jean's body, whose blood they had
sucked. They were tiny, secret hermits whose duty it was to
keep alive in those forests the memory of a young victim. They
were truly the living remains of my friend. I took care of them
as much as possible by not washing, not even scratching. At
times, I would pluck one of them out and hold it between my nail
and skin: I would examine it closely for a moment, with curiosity
and tenderness, and then replace it in my curly bush. Perhaps
their brothers were still living in Jean's hairs. The morgue
keeps bodies for a long time. (FUNERAL, pp. 41-42)

The sexual experience can become the measure of being. Glicksberg
observes, "If sexuality is an expression of life at its most intense, then it
is sex that defines the self."[39] For Genet's characters sex is indeed a
definer, though not the only one. When Our Lady is asked to defend
himself at his trial, he makes one of the most telling "statements" in all of
Genet's works. The murder of the old man is of little consequence because
he has become impotent: "The old guy was washed up. He couldn't even
get a hard-on" (LADY, p. 288). Sexual response for Our Lady is life's
only criterion.

If sexuality "defines the self," it may also at its most intense lead to
union with God. Rozanov, in fact, claims that

the tie of sex with God is stronger than the tie of intellect, and
even conscience, with God....

Because of its substance and function, sex belongs to the
transcendental and mystical order.... Sex transcends the limits
of nature, because it is anatural and supernatural.[40]

For Jean sexuality provides a circular course to union with God, but it
concomitantly allows for the hypostatization of sainthood. For Jean
transcending is descending. Canonization can be achieved through
abjection and mystical experience, to which sexuality is a prelude. Knapp
is even more explicit: "Divinity can be reached both through spirituality

and sexuality. For Genet, they are one."[41] Genet resolves the conflict between "instinctual demands" and a desire for transcendence by simply combining them.

Jean fervently desires canonization, but he is rather like Eliot's Beckett who does "the right deed for the wrong reason." Jean does the wrong deed for the wrong reason. His concept of sanctity is naturally diametrically opposed to the Christological. William James lists the following charateristics of universal saintliness:

1. A wider life than the mundane

2. Surrender to friendly ideal power

3. Elation and freedom as selfhood melts

4. An attitude of love and positive response to the non-ego

5. As "practical consequences": asceticism, strength of soul, purity, charity.[42]

It would be superfluous to depict each of these characteristics as it occurs in transvalued form in Genet's world. Suffice it to say that although there is a startling similarity in what James terms "practical consequences," asceticism becomes abjection and degradation but not continence, and charity is not an authentic relationship with those who are loathsome for their sakes, but rather a dehumanized attachment to the loathsomeness itself. Jean craves sanctity to affirm his "special destiny." "I was an illegitimate child," says Genet. "I was outside the social order. What could I wish for, if not for a special destiny? ... The only thing left for me was to want to be a saint, just that; in other words, a negation of man."[43] Genet-become-Jean negates humanity. Sanctity is not the highest ideal; rather negation is, and it can only be achieved by descending; humanity is left behind, and Jean immerses himself in abjection and evil.

Even sanctity is an excuse for absolute moral solitude, but it is the image most frequently employed. One of the most powerful examples of another possible destiny achieved through abjection (although this too might be termed sainthood) is a Uranian existence:

> The atmosphere of the planet Uranus appears to be so heavy that the ferns there are creepers; the animals drag along, crushed by the weight of the gases. I want to mingle with these humiliated creatures which are always on their bellies. If metempsychosis should grant me a new dwelling place, I choose that forlorn planet, I inhabit it with the convicts of my race. Amidst hideous reptiles, I pursue an eternal, miserable death in a darkness where the leaves will be black, the waters of the marshes thick and cold. Sleep will be denied me. On the contrary, I recognize, with increasing lucidity, the unclean fraternity of the smiling alligators. (JOURNAL, p. 45)

Normally, however, abjection is posited in degradating terms, such as betrayal, filth, lice, crabs, hunger, and mendicancy--combined paradoxically with incontinence. Darling "liked selling out on people, for this dehumanized him. Dehumanizing myself is my most fundamental tendency" (LADY, p. 82). Divine "cut off her lashes so as to be even more repulsive" (LADY, p. 294). Or Jean becomes a begger: "My life of poverty in Spain was a kind of degradation, a fall involving shame"; "I abased myself further. I no longer begged for money but for scraps of food" (JOURNAL, pp. 46, 79). "The Spain of beggers, of shameful and humiliated poverty" (JOURNAL, p. 256), produces sanctity. Suffering and degradation allow Jean to villify his body, which is synonymous with beautifying the spirit. Yet transcendence is descendence, and Jean is "ascetic" or "charitable" on his own terms. Repulsiveness becomes an end in itself, so that ultimately it is possible to say, not that abjection leads to sanctity (the typical position), but that abjection is sanctity. Cioran, the French philospher, empathizes with Jean's aspirations:

Carpathian shepherds have made a much deeper impressionon on me than the professors of Germany, the wits of Paris. I have seen Spanish beggers and I should like to have been their hagiographer. They had no need to invent a life for themselves: they existed; which does not happen in civilization.[44]

Ricoeur indicates that under normal circumstances evil allows for the triadic progression from defilement to sin and guilt.[45] Thus evil (and abjection in a literal sense) is contamination; it is a stain and hence a sin; the process produces guilt, which should logically lead to expiation. For Genet's characters criminal acts, abjection, and suffering are indeed defilement and perhaps even sin, though sin as "alienation from oneself" (Ricoeur) would be difficult to defend given Sartre's contention that these characters are affirming themselves through contamination. Perhaps Sartre is confusing existential choice with psychological need; sincere beliefs with inauthentic, excapist action. Guilt and expiation, at any rate, are of no significance to Genet. Instead an anagogical transposition occurs that takes no account of psychological reactions (see Figure 4).

Figure 4. Sin and Sainthood in Genet's World

```
                          Guilt------Expiation
        Defilement-----Sin----                    ---Sainthood
```

This leap from defilement/sin to sanctity is comprehensible if one understands that sanctity and contamination are in Genet's world one and the same: "The sacredness of humiliation lies in the actual experience of humiliation, which is therefore not so much a means to an end, as an end in itself--or at least it is inseparable from, and simultaneous with that end."[46] It would be more consistent to say, not that humiliation or abjection or evil and sanctity are synonymous, but that all those are means to achieve <u>absolute</u> uniqueness, Jean's essence, the narcissistic deity. It is this uniqueness that is synonymous with sainthood.

Humiliation, shame, and suffering are unpleasant attributes of being. To avoid them may be to escape from the human condition. Yet to affirm them as Jean does is also an escape from reality. This is doubly true, because Jean's avowed end is "solitude," outside the human sphere. Jean demands a suffering existence: "I have no right to be joyful. Laughter desecrates my suffering" (FUNERAL, p. 167); "I would have liked my suffering to be greater" (FUNERAL, p. 55); "I took upon myself his shame and suffering" (MIRACLE, p. 103). There are two aspects to suffering to be considered. Philosophically, suffering is acclaimed; and Genet is obviously following Nietzsche's suggestion: "Profound suffering makes noble; it separates."[47] Through self-denegration uniqueness, solitude, and sanctity may be achieved. It is this very hope that Baudelaire articulates:

> --Soyez béni, mon Dieu, qui donnez la souffrance
> Comme un divin remède à nos impuretés
> Et comme la meilleure et la plus essence
> Qui prépare les forts aux saintes voluptés!

Yet, from a psychological point of view, the pursuit of extreme suffering is an indication of pathology. Horney observes that the neurotic desires suffering, suffers "more than the average person," and "suffers more than is warranted by reality."[48] Excessive suffering consequently must be viewed as another manifestation of pathology, the philosophical view notwithstanding.

Jean's pragmatic approach to sanctity--"saintliness means turning pain to good account" (JOURNAL, p. 205)--necessitates renunciation, the cultivation of those ascetic qualities listed above. At times, Jean admits to an ambiguous attitude, saying, for example, "Though saintliness is my goal,

I cannot tell what it is" (JOURNAL, p. 208). More frequently, however, he adumbrates sanctity in terms of process and solitude. Uniqueness for Jean is absolute egregiousness: living "according to Heaven, in spite of God" (MIRACLE, p. 46). Yet an internalized "heaven" demands abjection and evil, which result in solitude, that is, sanctity. Our Lady, Divine, and Riton unconsciously reach this state of perfection. Jean never admits that he does so, except through his alter egos.

Sanctity is apparently as dependent on murder (the canonized are invariably murderers) as on internalizing God:

> God: my inner tribunal
> Saintliness: union with God.
> (JOURNAL, p. 245)

Here Jean, like Sartre, confuses existential choice with psychological need. He implies that a state of moral perfection will exist when he is at one with himself. He refuses to acknowledge the possibility that his inner demands are compulsive, uncontrollable, or distorted. From a theological point of view (excluding the perverseness of Genet's vision), what he attempts is untenable. Although "God has consigned all men to disobedience, that he may have mercy upon all" (Romans 11:32), achieving grace through the "cultivation of sin" is unacceptable. Ricoeur notes: "No one can make a technique out of it and pretend that he sins abundantly in order that grace may superabound."[49] It would appear that this is true even for Jean apotheosized.

The foregoing is Genet's vision of the world. The emphasis has been axio-ethical, the perspective pathological. Within Genet's world innumerable objects, actions, concepts, and forces are significant, but they only bear on the pathological aspect insofar as they are "excessive." It would be beyond the scope of this essay to discuss symbols, objects, gestures, and so on, though these clearly do play an important role. One final comment concerning death, however, is essential.

Coe comments, "Simone de Beauvoir envisages the negativity of death as the only force strong enough to create positive significance in life."[50] Heidegger insists that man is "thrown" into a world whose primary significator is death; it is death that allows life to be meaningful. For Genet death brings finality. Sainthood is process and solitude, not nonbeing; death negates consciousness, which is mandatory for perception. Others, of course, can look back on the saintly character of an executed Harcamone or Bulkaen, but they can no longer experience sainthood's mystical beauty. Death is an extremely frequent occurrence: murderers kill and are in turn executed, soldiers destroy, children and prisoners fight to the end, and so on. Death for Genet is both significance and negation. It is toward death that his characters move; once the end is achieved, however, there can be nothing further.

The characters one meets in Genet's fiction continually manifest pathological traits, indications that their view of the universe is distorted, at times even grotesque. Murder and theft are ritualistic; insignificant gestures become more important than they should be; superficial (even social) appearance is more consequential than actuality--the mask as opposed to the leprosy that it covers, in Genet's terms. James's descripiton of the psychopath is an apposite conclusion to this study because Genet's characters conform to it in every detail:

> In the pschopathic temperament we have the emotionality which is the sine qua non of moral perception; we have the intensity and tendency to emphasis which are the essence of practical moral vigor; and we have the love of metaphysics and mysticism which carry one's interests beyond the surface of the sensible world.[51]

2. LOUIS-FERDINAND CÉLINE: EVIL OBSERVED

> "And yet there is some good in
> the world," replied Candide.
> "Maybe," said Martin, "but it has
> escaped my knowledge."
>
> --Voltaire

The pathology of Céline's vision differs significantly from that of Genet. Genet's characters insist upon evil, search it out, create it, and ultimately apotheosize the unpleasant, the revolting, and the heinous, whereas Céline's protagonist, Ferdinand, is a picaresque moralist who simply observes a world blackened by ugliness, sordidness, and evil as he stumbles from one encounter to another. While for Céline the world is ethically bifurcate, Ferdinand's periphery is limited to the evil aspect. The good exists, but it is an infrequent occurrence. Ferdinand might be called an involved observer; he plays a seminal role in his multitudinous adventures and experiences, but he nonetheless remains at a distance, aloof at times, and comments philosophically, sociologically, and ethically on what he observes. Because invariably he perceives the unpleasant, his picture of the world is distorted; he depicts the world almost exclusively in pessimistic terms. Yet evil for Céline is externalized. Acting as an undiscriminating roving camera, Ferdinand records whatever he perceives. This material may later be edited, but Ferdinand's purview of the world ramains arbitrary and discursive.

Ferdinand's position is rather complex. On the one hand, he approbates the Judaeo-Christian ethic, and implies that he possesses a desire for the good, his own as well as mankind's. On the other hand, he remains indifferent to the plight of the individuals whom he encounters for fear of disturbing his invariably precarious economic status or because he simply does not wish to become involved. All of his ethical action can be imputed to the fluctuating paranoia that haunts him. Ferdinand is not paranoid because he believes that someone is dedicated to his destruction; rather, through a kind of Pavlovian reinforcement, he has come to believe that man is evil and will use other beings as means rather than ends. He is fearful of man in general because of his particular experiences. Thus Céline's vision of the universe is based on a blunder in logic: he reasons from a limited particular to a limited general and holds his inductions to be ubiquitously valid since he concludes that the world is abhorrent and man is "arrested putrescence."

Ferdinand is a Manichee gone beserk, but paradoxically he avoids the kinds of actions that so influence his own perspective. With few exceptions he remains upright, meritorious, and even compassionate. Only infrequently does he act asocially or in a flagrantly evil fashion, and he more than compensates for those incidents by his general altruism and benevolence. Although such a depiction of Céline's world is unusual, it is nonetheless valid. Ferdinand suffers from a multitude of pathological manifestations, for example, insecurity, paranoia, hallucinations, extreme indifference, and various obsessions, but the pathology of Céline's vision is nonetheless exterior to Ferdinand. Although Ferdinand may not be well, the world he perceives is moribund.

In order to understand fully the pathological nature of Céline's vision, it is necessary to consider the way in which he structures his fiction. The novels are composed of a multitude of distinct incidents held together by the narrative of the protagonist, Ferdinand. Each novel is part of a broader panorama, which may be viewed generally as the story of Ferdinand's entire life. We will consider his youth (DEATH ON THE INSTALLMENT PLAN), his adolescence and young adulthood (JOURNEY TO

THE END OF THE NIGHT), a short respite in England (GUIGNOL'S BAND), and some later experiences during the Second World War (CASTLE TO CASTLE). The chronological continuity in this sequence cannot be ignored.

No basic a priori metaphysic lies at the core of Céline's vision. Instead his excessively cynical and pessimistic view emerges as Ferdinand moves from one situation to another. Ferdinand does not begin with preconceived notions concerning man and his universe; his beliefs develop as one experience reinforces the next. (This pattern is even more evident if one considers THE LIFE AND WORK OF SEMMELWEISS--Ostrovsky does--for in that work Céline manifests the positive half of existence.) Ferdinand is a modern picaro: a sensitive, impressionistic, philosophic intellectual who lives by his wits and skill and who extricates himself from one unpleasant situation only to discover himself entangled in another. The web is continuous; there is almost no respite. Céline achieves an excellent union of the realistic picaro, such as Defoe's Robinson Crusoe or Moll Flanders, and the hyperbolic creatures that one finds in Rabelais, Voltaire, and Cervantes. Ferdinand is a picaro sensitive and intelligent enough to relate actual occurrences, but at the same time, because of his psychological unbalance, he portrays a disoriented, bizarre and at times grotesque world analogous to that of Voltaire's CANDIDE or Cervantes.

Céline's method is similar to Voltaire's. They both disclaim optimistic blindness. They both hyperbolically depict the ills of mankind through a sarcasm that is grotesque in its extreme manifestations. Yet Céline is far more powerful, far more disturbing than Voltaire because he also employs the method of Defoe, who insists on an exacting verisimilitude. Hence Céline's rendering of war's horrors, analogous to Goya's DESASTRES DE LA GUERRA, is revolting, horrifying, and must lead to despair:

> They were in each other's arms and would continue the
> embrace for ever, but the cavalryman hadn't his head any
> more, only his neck open at the top with blood bubbling in it like
> stew in a pot. The colonel's stomach was slit open and he was
> making an ugly face about that. It must have been painful when
> that happened. So much the worse for him. If he'd gone away
> when the firing began, he wouldn't have had it.
>
> All this heap of flesh was bleeding like the deuce. Shells
> were still bursting to right and left of the picture. (JOURNEY,
> p. 13)

Voltaire's hyperbole is so intense that it is amusing. In fact, his tone demands an amused response rather than abhorrence: "The entertainment began by a discharge of cannons, which in the twinkling of an eye, laid flat about 6,000 men on each side. The musket bullets swept away, out of the best of all possible worlds, 9 or 10,000 scoundrels that infested its surface" (CANDIDE, chapter 3). Voltaire's satire has a distancing effect even when the descriptions are vivid and presumably horrible. By skirting both extremes, that is, Defoe's unmitigated realism (for example, in JOURNAL OF THE PLAGUE YEAR) and Voltaire's sarcasm, Céline succeeds in creating a credibly grotesque universe that is inhabited by a picaresque hero unparalleled in the history of literature.

The term picaro cannot serve here as a simplifying concept because Ferdinand's complexity precludes that. Structurally, Ferdinand provides the link that allows the sequence of incidents and ultimately of the novels to be viewed as a coherent whole. Céline's entire opus is a painstaking unveiling of the Ferdinand saga, in the manner of Galsworthy or Mann. In BUDDENBROOKS, for example, one follows the decadence of a family from generation to generation. Similarly, Céline permits the reader to follow Ferdinand's precarious movement toward inevitable death. Ferdinand's degeneration is simply a mirror reflection of the putrifying world.

Thus, on the one hand, Céline's protagonist serves the usual picaresque purpose of structural unifier. Yet, on the other hand, he is a character of such complexity, despite his ostensible superficiality, that a valid comparison may be drawn between him and Dostoevsky's Underground Man. Round and dynamic (rather than flat and static), Ferdinand presents to the world an indifferent if not malicious visage that upon careful scrutiny is seen to be simply a mask protecting this sensitive and compassionate creature from the abominations of his surroundings, where poverty, horror, and evil never relinquish their hold. If Ferdinand can only infrequently actualize goodness, that is, affirm the good through personal action, he is nonetheless conscious and approbative of its presence in others, be it in the prostitute Molly, the colonialist Alcide, or his relative Édouard.

Generally, although Ferdinand appears to be indifferent, he is actually compassionate; although he frequently affirms evil, he attempts to do good and recognizes goodness in others. These rather controversial statements would seem to nullify much of what has been said in Ferdinand's defense, but that is not the case at all. The etiology of Ferdinand's ethical position, and more particularly of his "evil" actions, makes it patently clear that he has become indifferent as a defense against the world's stupidity and evil, and only upon extreme provocation. For example, his presumptive murder of the dwarf in GUIGNOL's BAND is the result of paranoia brought on by blatant betrayal. Moreover, he is far more interested in saving his own neck, than in malicious revenge, though the latter is certainly a motive. Whereas Genet's protagonist, Jean, demands and creates an evil private microcosm, Ferdinand finds himself trapped in an evil world for which he cannot be held culpable. If he allows his surroundings to impinge upon him and ultimately cause him to act maliciously, he nonetheless persistently implies his disapprobation of the world as it is and of his own actions as well. The world is evil, not Ferdinand, and thus Céline's pathological vision is paradoxically to be found not in his protagonist but rather in the world that he so minutely depicts. Ferdinand too is ill, but one must distinguish between Ferdinand and the world at large, between the involved observer and that which he observes.

Because Céline believes that the entire world is pathological, unlike the limited and purposively created pathology of Genet, one may feel that Céline paints a more dismal picture of the human condition. His extreme pessimism, at times totally nihilistic, is inexorable. Yet his hyperbolic distortion of human experience is founded on valid assumptions that are derived from valid, though limited, experience. Conversely, Genet's universe is personal, self-aggrandizing, compulsive, escapist, and absolutely dehumanizing. Because Céline's world is preferable, Hindus asserts that Ferdinand in JOURNEY is meritorious: "In JOURNEY, after all, underneath everything the sensitive reader is aware of the sensitivity and morality of Ferdinand."[1] This is generally true for Céline's entire vision, and in fact, Hindus refers to Céline's "basically hopeful nature."[2] Hayman is even more generous when he indicates that "there lingers in his books an underlying concern for humanity."[3] This subtly intimated "concern for humanity" redeems Céline's pessimistic vituperation. The world, Ferdinand discovers, is abhorrent, but that does not plunge him into eternal nihilistic despair. Instead, Ferdinand affirms the validity of human existence through his individualistic, existential actions--the actions of his complex life as a picaro, apprentice, soldier, adventurer, worker, and doctor to the poor.

There are basically only two positions from which one may develop a pessimistic <u>Weltanschauung</u>. If one does not suffer but observes evil and suffering in others, one may conclude that the world is primarily evil, one's own good fortune notwithstanding. Or one may personally partake of the world's misery and consequently develop a generally pessimistic <u>Weltanschauung</u> from a particular set of experiences. The latter is the more usual sequence of events, and it is in that manner that men like Heine and Leopardi arrive at their dreary pictures of the human condition. "Arcano è tutto,/Fuor che il nostro dolor," admonishes Leopardi. Ferdinand, from his earliest experiences, is both a personal sufferer and an observer of the world gone mad. He is impecunious, unhappy, and harassed by his fanatical parents. In adulthood, sickness and pain are added to his burdens. The world that he observes is a reflection of his personal experiences and is characterized by hypocrisy, self-seeking, blatant stupidity, callousness, ugliness, and death. Ferdinand portrays this inexorably grotesque world to us and only as his experiences mount up and reinforce one another does his rather simple pessimism emerge: humanity inhabits "a truly appalling, awful world."

Thus Céline's fiction consists of variations on a theme. It is extremely repetitive; although the actual experiences that are related may differ, the perspective is invariably the same. Céline's fictional world has the superficial quality associated with Hemingway; the earthy adventures of the downtrodden are narrated in direct colloquial language, as in TO HAVE AND HAVE NOT. If Céline takes a metaphysical position, it is simplistic and emerges only as the protagonist experiences and suffers.

Tsanoff, discussing Julius Bahnsen, observes, "The only pessimism worthy of the name is a pessimism tragically earnest and at the same time grimly humorous."[4]   The ostensible pessimism of the Romantics, especially

that of the Germans, such as Novalis and Goethe's Werther, is extremely

diluted, sentimental Sehnsucht: "die blaue Blume" or suicide for love

satisfies the yearning.   At the core of that world lies ambiguity, not

ugliness.   Heine, however, is like Céline, both "tragically earnest" and

"grimly humorous":

> Und Fratzenbilder nur und sieche Schatten
> Seh' ich auf dieser Erde, und ich weiss nicht,
> Ist sie ein Tollhaus oder Krankenhaus.

The truly pessimistic Weltanschauung has madness and disease at its

core.   Even naturalists minutely depicting life's sordid elements are

basically not pessimists.   A composite pessimistic Weltanschauung would

include Schopenhauer's philosophical perspective limned by Bosch,

Brueghel, and Goya and danced by Ghelderode to lugubrious Wagnerian

strains.   Céline achieves a synthesis of the mundane, pessimistic, and

grotesquely comic, and the potency of the mix is unequaled in West,

Ghelderode, Albee, or even Beckett.

Man is the most offensive of creatures:

> [He] is made of dust, of mud, of ashes; worse yet, of the
> foulest seed; conceived in the itch of the flesh, in the heat of
> passion, in the stench of lust; and worse, in the depths of sin;
> born to labor, to dolor, to horror; more miserable still, to
> death.   He acts wickedly, offending God, offending his
> neighbor, offending himself; he acts infamously, polluting fame,
> polluting conscience, polluting character; he acts vainly
> neglecting the serious, neglecting the useful, neglecting the
> necessary.   He is food for fire ever blazing and burning
> unquenched; food for worms, ever gnawing and eating without
> end; a mass of putrescence, ever noisome and horribly foul.[5]

That is Céline's evaluation of homo sapiens, but in fact, it was not written

by him, but by Pope Innocent III at the end of the twelfth century.   The

pope was castigating the sordid and repulsive aspects of his fellow

creatures who presumably had been created in the image of God.   The medieval ethos perhaps demanded such extreme pessimism while conversely the church provided the spiritual basis for extreme optimism. That Innocent III could be so vituperative mitigates to a certain extent Céline's pessimistic picture of human existence--but only insignificantly, since the medieval Christian, when all was said and done, had the hope of redemption after death. For Céline the only redemption is death itself.

Ferdinand's early life consists of poverty, hunger, beatings, and family scenes--brawls between his crippled, limping mother and a raving, paranoid father. His grandmother too has her problems. That mode of existence sets the pattern for Ferdinand's existential reactions. Harassed by an oppressive environment, he is forced to set up defense mechanisms: he becomes variously stupid, selfish, indifferent, malicious, paranoid, and evil. Yet he is simply a reflection, even a parody, of his own experiences. He is shaped and unduly influenced by an environment that is almost invariably malevolent, an environment inhabited by diseased beings who suffer from instability, insecurity, and compulsions. It is no surprise that he ultimately develops into a caricature of the pathological creatures around him. As Horney points out,

> It seems that the person who is likely to become neurotic is one who has experienced the culturally determined difficulties in an accentuated form, mostly through the medium of childhood experiences, and who has consequently been unable to solve them, or has solved them only at great cost to his personality. We might call him a stepchild of our culture.[6]

With few exceptions Ferdinand encounters no whole, balanced people; if those whom he meets are not clinically ill or socially aberrant, then they are ludicrous distortions--buffoons, grotesques, or raving maniacs.

Even Ferdinand's earliest memories are of life's sewer. There is never a respite, a moment of joy, or a pleasant family experience. His tyrannical

father makes life unpleasant in the evenings, and during the day Ferdinand
spends his time either with his mother in their junk shop or racing around
Paris and its environs selling and delivering bits of lace and assorted trash
to the rich. Not only is he subjected as a young child to the sexual
practices of his parents and the neighbors, he is also kissed, caressed,
and manhandled by relatives and customers. On an evening delivery with
his father he is lured into a bedroom:

> The lady gives me a piece of candy. I follow her into the
> bedroom. The maid comes in too. The lady lies down in a
> mess of lace. All of a sudden she hikes up her dressing gown
> and shows me her fat legs, her behind, and her clump of hair.
> Whew! She goes poking around inside with her fingers ...
>
> "Come, little darling! ... Come, little love! ... Come,
> suck me in there! ..." Her voice was ever so soft and tender,
> no one had ever spoken to me like that before. She opens it
> out. Oozing.
>
> The maid was doubled up with laughter. That's what held
> me back. I ran off to the kitchen. I wasn't crying anymore.
> (DEATH, p. 59)[7]

It would be surprising indeed if early sexual experiences of this sort,
which may be termed psychological rapes, did not leave a lasting impression
on a child hardly old enough to read or to take care of his personal
hygiene. Like Stephen Daedalus, Ferdinand comes to be plagued by sexual
practices that are forced upon him or freely chosen. His frequent onanism,
for example, is more an escape from his dreary existence than a pleasurable
experience. Unlike Daedalus, Ferdinand manifests little fear, little remorse,
and little contrition. He is a hardened cynic at a very tender age.

A few years later, Ferdinand has a similar and more exaggerated
sexual encounter with an older and fatter woman, the wife of his employer.
At first he simply observes her outlandish lovemaking, but then he is once
again lured into the bedroom. This time he is literally forced into

copulation. The ugly, automatic sexual usage is entirely destructive.

Love, respect, and even passion are absent:

> I didn't dare take off too much. Just the choker that was killing
> me ... and my coat and vest ... she hung them up beside the
> bed, on the back of the chair ... I didn't want to take
> everything off ... the way Antoine did ... I knew my ass was
> shitty and my feet coalblack ... I could smell myself ... to keep
> her from insisting, I started up again as fast as I could ... I
> played the ardent lover, I climbed, I squeezed, I grunted.
> (DEATH, p. 181)

There is no indication that Ferdinand finds the encounter enjoyable. In

fact, the very antithesis is implied:

> "Oh, what a little beast!" she hollers. "Oh, what a slimy little
> toad! ... Come quick and let me clean you up ..." She goes for
> my pecker ... she makes a meal of it ... she likes the sauce ...
> "Oh, what a delicious little dessert!" she squeals. She goes
> looking for it all over my legs ... she pokes into the folds ...
> she's really thorough ... she's going to swoon again ... she's
> down on her knees, clinging to my legs, she contracts, she
> relaxes ... fat ass and all, she's as nimble as a cat. She forces
> me down on her again ... "I'll show you, you little louse," she
> says roguishly. She sticks two fingers into my opening. She
> forces me. What a scrimmage! The stinker, the way she's
> steamed up, she'll be at it all day! (DEATH, p. 182)

That Céline is condemned for his revoltingly detailed depictions of life in

the sewer is rather more comprehensible than the censure that Ferdinand's

actions evoke. For Ferdinand is young, naive, and hardly culpable. In

fact, he finds the situation equally repulsive. He is caught; he is

involved; but his reactions are an implicit condemnation of the woman, his

own actions, and the social values involved:

> "Wait for me, angel," she sings out ... I've had enough. I jump
> into my suit ... I grab the door, I push it open, I'm on the
> landing ... I take the stairs four at a time ... I take a good
> deep breath ... I'm out in the street ... It's time to think things
> over ... I catch my breath ... I walk slowly toward the
> boulevards. (DEATH, p. 182)

As it turns out, the woman has stolen a jewel from him during their sexual

exercise, and the theft causes him a great deal of trouble and torment.

64

The damage has been done, and all of his later sexual experiences fall into the destructive-usage category. It is as if a pattern has been set in motion and must be repeated ad infinitum: in quick succession follow the fritter girl, the children at Meanwell, and the distracted Nora Merrywin. In CASTLE TO CASTLE, Ferdinand's wife is never spoken of in sexual terms, and Molly is discovered in a Detroit brothel. It is perhaps with this benevolent prostitute, however, that Ferdinand achieves his purest relationship with another human being. Dostoevsky's Underground Man uses and destroys his friendly whore; his actions are heinous. Although Ferdinand respects Molly, he simply leaves her, perhaps because he is unaccustomed to too much joy.

Ferdinand's maniacal father, Auguste, takes out his frustrations, delusions, and paranoia on both his wife and son. Ferdinand therefore spends much of his time excusing himself: "I apologized for everything I did, I was always apologizing. [...] In the end I'd always apologize for my insolence ... it was an act, I hadn't done anything" (DEATH, pp. 55, 63). The father is like a sensitive land mine; at the slightest provocation he will lose all touch with reality. On one notable occasion a customer steals a handkerchief:

> "What's that?" He couldn't take it in. "You didn't say anything? You let them get away with it? The fruits of our toil!" He was in such a rage that he cracked at the seams. His jacket burst. "It's abominable!" he roared. In spite of the uproar my mother kept yelping some kind of excuses ... he had stopped listening. He seized his knife and brought it down in the middle of his plate ... it split, the noodle juice ran all over the place. "No, no! I can't stand it." He rushed around, waving his arms. He took hold of the little sideboard, the Henri III. He shook it like a plum tree. There was an avalanche of dishes. (DEATH, p. 66)

There is something pathetically comic about this bellowing lunatic in the midst of the ubiquitous noodle juice, destroying quantities of possessions for the sake of a bit of stolen lace. But the comic aspect is soon

dissipated as he thoroughly thrashes his wife:

"Auguste! Auguste! Stop!" And then short stifled gasps ...

> I come part of the way down to look ... He's dragging her
> along the banister. She hangs on. She clutches his neck.
> That's what saves her. It's he who pulls loose ... he pushes her
> over. She somersaults ... she bounces down the stairs ... I can
> hear the dull thuds ... At the bottom she picks herself up ...
> then he takes a powder ... he leaves through the shop ... he
> goes out in the street. She struggles to her feet ... she goes
> back to the kitchen. She has blood in her hair. She washes at
> the sink ... she's sobbing ... she gags ... she sweeps up the
> breakage ... He comes home very late on these occasions ...
> everything is very quiet again. (DEATH, p. 67)

The loss of the jewel mentioned above results in an enduring "psychosis":

> My father talked to himself ... he went off into monologues ...
> raging and fuming ... he went on and on ... about the forces of
> evil ... his whole repertory ... Destiny ... The Jews ... his
> rotten luck ... The Exposition ... Providence ... The Freemasons
> ... (DEATH, pp. 187-88)

The situation cannot continue, and one night Ferdinand, guilty of wasting

five francs, is lacerated to such an extent that he can no longer control

himself. "This slimy viper!" howls Auguste. "He's after our hide. He's

always been plotting against us!" (DEATH, p. 316). Ferdinand, the family

scapegoat, finally expiates the years of torment:

> ... just one jump ... I'm over him. I lift up the big heavy
> machine ... I lift it way up. And wham! ... I give it to him full
> in the face! He hasn't got time to parry ...

> ... I punch him on the ground ... he bellows ... he
> gurgles ... that'll do. I dig into the fat on his neck ... I'm on
> my knees on top of him ... I'm tangled up in his bandages ...
> both my hands are caught. I pull. I squeeze. He's still
> groaning ... he's wriggling ... I weigh down on him ... he's
> disgusting ... he squawks ... I pound him ... I massacre him
> ... I'm squatting down ... I dig into the meat ... it's soft ...
> he's drooling ... (DEATH, p. 316)

He is forced to leave home.

66

It is clear that his sordid early environment, including his raving father and the grotesque sexual practices of various acquaintances, detrimentally influences Ferdinand's perspective. He grows bitter, callous, and indifferent, and justifiably so as a defense against pain and frustration. Intimacies only lead to further suffering, and Ferdinand catalogues all of the problems of his youth, rationalizing his lack of involvement but concomitantly indicating preconscious causes for his apparently heinous desires and actions:

> it cramped my cock to think of it ... of all the treachery of things ... as soon as you let anybody wrap you up ... the whole stinking rotten business ... and of my mother ... ah, the poor woman! And of Gorloge and Madame Méhon and the quotations! And the kitchen faucet! And Lavelongue! And little André! The whole lousy mess! Yes, damn it all, I had as much as I could take ... a big stinking steaming load of shit up to here ... (DEATH, p. 215)

A warped world produces warped progeny. The world as Ferdinand perceives it is evil and diseased, filled with filth and suffering. This is reflected in Ferdinand in varying degrees at different times. As an adolescent he is totally disgusted and therefore extremely cynical, coarse, and malicious (though it is necessary to reiterate in Ferdinand's defense that his reaction is commensurate with its cause). As he matures, he has some less cynical, or indifferent, moments; incidents of goodness and charity, in fact, are not uncommon. As an adolescent, however, he is only capable of harsh reactions: he just cannot afford to trust others; he has been betrayed too often. Nora Merrywin is patient and kind, but Ferdinand is so afraid of goodness that he simply concludes, "Women are scum." The young fritter girl's thoughtfulness evokes a similar sentiment:

> Wasn't I hungry? She offered to get me something to eat, her heart really seemed to be in the right place ... Dazed as I was, I wondered if I'd have the strength to topple her off the edge with

a good swift kick in the ass. Well, how about it? (DEATH, p. 216)

The point is that by the time Ferdinand has reached adolescence his experiences have reinforced his earliest impressions to such an extent that he demonstrates an ontology of evil. Tsanoff's philosophical clarification of evil provides the key to Ferdinand's pessimism:

> Evil and the problem of evil seem to arise from an experienced clash and disaccord of the actuality with the ideal, whatever this may be. The consciousness of this frustration may be so intense as to lead to a settled conviction that the clash and disaccord are irremediable, that frustration is the primal and the final fact of life. This conviction, if reasoned, provides the texture of pessimistic philosophy, which may go to such an extreme painful sense of despised actuality that the cherished ideal is pronounced illusory, the world is conceived in terms which consistently preclude the reality of positive worth. Evil, in such a philosophy of despair, becomes the fundamental reality.[8]

The ideal is external to Ferdinand's world; the disaccord is all he ever knows. He is in a constant state of frustration, anxiety, and despair, yet no pessimistic ontology is formally articulated. Instead Ferdinand depicts a series of experiences, examples, and execrations that must be codified by the reader. Céline is not a philosopher, not even a philosophical novelist. He portrays an ontological core in his works only in the similarity of the experiences that he conveys. In that respect evil is indeed "the fundamental reality" for Céline and despair is a common occurrence.

Yet despair paradoxically acts as a redeeming factor for Ferdinand. At the end of his adolescence he formulates a new attitude toward human beings and the world, an attitude that is more dormant than active but continues to manifest itself subtly in a general fashion. This new dimension is Ferdinand's social consciousness, his desire for social amelioration. It is ludicrous indeed to claim as one critic does that Beckett's despair is actually its antithesis; that for Beckett men are not the groveling creatures that Vladimir, Hamm, and Malone appear to be, that those characters actually affirm man's potentiality and excellence. To insist on a social consciousness in Céline's world would be a misinterpretation as well. Yet, concomitantly, to avoid Ferdinand's good points is flagrantly erroneous. Beneath all of the pessimistic appraisals, the nihilistic declamations, the egomaniacal jeremiads runs a positive current of affirmation. That is Tillich's "courage of despair." Tillich declares, "Man has lost a meaningful world and a self which lives in meanings out of a spiritual center." Nonetheless, he continues, "He is still man enough to experience his dehumanization as despair."[9] Although Ferdinand's despairing affirmation is tempered with caustic cynicism, he is not an unmitigated cynic.

After his abortive experiences with the maniacal Courtial, at the outset of JOURNEY TO THE END OF THE NIGHT, Ferdinand, for all of his cynical scoffing, enlists in the army. Much that he has known before is confirmed while working for Courtial, but the new life still allows him some respite from the sordidness of the Passage des Bérésinas and the raving of his father. The vitriolic scenes at Courtial's are amusing in comparison with those of his youth. While reinforcing his pessimistic proclivity, the extended vacation at Courtial's also allows him to mellow. The young adult first presented in JOURNEY is not quite as paranoid, distrustful, and self-seeking as Courtial's apprentice. Thus, although he satirically denigrates meaningfulness, the French, Nationalism, and War, he is a student of medicine prior to his enlistment. Both of those pursuits, soldiering and doctoring, ultimately prove disillusioning, but at this time in Ferdinand's life they augur change, progress, and amelioration.

In the army Ferdinand is immediately caught up in a new form of socially acceptable madness, one that he neither comprehends nor advocates. His war experiences are related sarcastically, and, though at times the exaggeration tends toward parody, the absurdities depicted are not merely possible. There is every indication that they are typical: spoiled hedonistic generals; ludicrous orders; wanton, gory destruction. The four weeks recounted seem like four years. This repeats the earlier pattern: open to new affirmative experiences, Ferdinand discovers only madness and horror. Philosophically, his preconceived notions concerning the human condition are reinforced. Psychologically, the pathological responses of various people influence him detrimentally. Yet in the army he meets the only real friend he ever has. Robinson, a moral cripple, is an extremely unsavory and troublesome person, but his moral apathy serves to accentuate Ferdinand's negative goodness. In other words, as the murders and pillage of the Germans are a direct contrast to Ferdinand's polite request for a bottle of wine, so is Robinson's heinous behavior and moral indifference a contrast to Ferdinand's attempts to achieve a modicum of goodness. Hindus alleges that "Céline wants to do good and can do nothing but evil."[10] Ferdinand too desires the good, but unlike Céline he does not always propagate evil. Although he is surrounded by stupidity and ugliness, he continues to fight against them. He never totally capitulates. This frustrated goodness distinguishes Ferdinand from almost everyone whom he meets.

I have been insisting, first, on the moral turpitude of Céline's world and, second, on Ferdinand's role as an involved observer who is influenced more by the evil than he would like to believe. It is as if Ferdinand, turning away from an especially unpleasant amputation, discovers that it is his own leg that has been removed. For all of his sarcasm and gory descriptions, he is not callous; he is not inured to the hideousness of life.

The butcher's residue--blood, fat, entrails, carcasses, and flies--is more than he can stomach: "I had to give way to an overwhelming desire to vomit--more than a little, until I fainted" (JOURNEY, p. 17).

The complexity of Ferdinand's personality, as indicated above, results in ambiguity. It is impossible to ascribe a static moral position to him. If he is repulsed at one moment, he may be jubilantly bizarre the next: "A pretty sight. You've no idea what a fine effect even the most insignificant little hamlet, which you wouldn't even notice in the daytime, in the dullest country, will make at night when it's burning" (JOURNEY, p. 25). The line is extremely fine between Céline's serious comments and his satirical thrusts, and at times it is difficult to distinguish one from the other. War itself is a manifestation of pathology propagated by automatons, and Ferdinand's evaluation is a covert attack on accepted social practices: one is "tortured and duped to death by a horde of vicious madmen, who had suddenly become incapable of doing anything else as long as they lived, but kill and be slit in half without knowing the reason why" (JOURNEY, p. 30). Ferdinand's defense is a simple, though general, cynicism that does not allow for authentic relationships with other people: "Lie, copulate and die. One wasn't allowed to do anything else" (JOURNEY, p. 50). He becomes something of a pariah, and all his relationships end in disaster. Lola, for example, or Musyne and later Molly are all alienated or abandoned.

Ferdinand's attempt to help others through doctoring, like his journeys to Africa and America, inexorably reaffirms "the madness of the world." He cannot contend with the insuperable stupidities of those whom he is attempting to help. Additionally, he is forced to demean himself before his poverty-stricken clientele for every franc he receives in payment. He becomes an embittered and disgusted man. Two incidents point up the stupidity with which he is faced. On one occasion he is called in to attend a young girl whose life is swiftly ebbing because of a botched abortion. He immediately suggests that the patient be taken to the hospital. Whereupon the mother replies: "What a disgrace! To the hospital, Doctor! What a disgrace for us! That is all that was needed--the last straw!" (JOURNEY, p. 259). As a doctor, Ferdinand is not indifferent to suffering, pain, and death, but he simply cannot cope with this mother's inconceivable attitude, and therefore he listens to her lamentations: "I again advised immediate removal to the hospital. More yelping, sharper still, more strident, more determined, in answer. Hopeless" (JOURNEY, p. 261). Ferdinand abandons hope, but he does not capitulate. He may not be able to abolish evil, but he avoids its perpetration. The second case also concerns a woman bleeding to death--from a miscarriage. She is surrounded by ludicrous, indifferent, and jabbering relatives and friends. Once again Ferdinand wishes to send her to the hospital, but no one can make a decision, least of all her obtuse husband. Ferdinand just leaves, and the woman presumably dies.

If actions are classed as moral, amoral, or immoral (good, indifferent, or evil), most of the people whom Ferdinand meets are immoral. Meanwhile he attempts to be moral, although at times he fails dismally. The few good creatures he encounters evoke maudlin approbation from him. Moral action in the external world is so infrequent an occurrence that he does not know how to cope with it, but his reaction is invariably incommensurate with his observation. Ferdinand's Uncle Édouard is probably the only entirely normal person in Céline's world who is also compassionate and moral. Perhaps he seems whole and authentic only because he appears at moments of crisis (as a deus ex machina) to rescue Ferdinand from the wrath of his parents. While Édouard is portrayed solely as a good man, most of the other characters on Céline's stage are depicted only in a grotesque light. They are presented in their immoral moments, because those are all that Ferdinand perceives. His observations are valid even if the ontological implications are not. His uncle's kindness generates discomfort: "It made me feel lousy to be sitting there like a sap, piling his groceries into my belly ... I was a skunk and I had my nerve with me ..." (DEATH, p. 324). Similarly, Alcide's sacrifices for his niece result in humility:

> He was so much better a man that I went very red in the face. Compared to Alcide, I was a useless ass, loutish and vain. There were no two ways about it.
>
> It wouldn't be a bad idea if there were something to distinguish good men from bad. (JOURNEY, pp. l59, l60)

And finally Molly, whose kindness, magnanimity, and respect are unique in Ferdinand's experience, forces him to manifest his inherent but atrophied moral consciousness. He abjures parasitism: "A last shred of decent feeling prevented me from making more out of this really much too lofty, generous nature, from speculating further on it" (JOURNEY, p. 229). Once again he is humbled: "I kissed Molly with all the fervour I had left in my wretched carcass. I was sad for once, really sad, sad for everybody, for myself, for her, for all men" (JOURNEY, p. 235).

Schopenhauer believed that "the absence of all egoistic motivation is ... the criterion of an action of moral worth" and further that "only insofar as an action has sprung from compassion does it have moral value."[11] With the exception of Édouard, Alcide, and Molly--the three benevolent people in Céline's gallery of immoral lunatics--Céline's characters are motivated by egoism, and they further their own interests through indifference, callousness, and malevolence. Evil individuals compositely form an evil society, and thus Ferdinand is faced with the insuperable immorality of the entire world. Niebuhr's point that moral man is seduced by an immoral society is especially germane.[12] Ferdinand, even after his unpleasant early life, is basically a moral creature, but since society continues to bombard him with horrors, it is difficult not to reciprocate in kind. The sensitive critic therefore perceives under Céline's veneer of filth, poverty, evil, and sarcasm a positive attitude toward good and a negative attitude toward evil.

Parker alleges that Céline

> makes us revise our moral values. It would be dishonest to deny that he is an anarchist--but his whole work is one long, sustained protest against that anarchy, that lawlessness into which the whole world finds itself plunged today.[13]

And Thiher, in essence, concurs:

> Céline is not attacking the values of civilization. To the contrary, he is appealing to the highest and most elementary values of our civilization in order to denounce the many forms of our corruption.[14]

Ferdinand's selfless, compassionate behavior on several occasions verifies those contentions. At Meanwell he is recalcitrant and uncooperative--"I'm hardened, take it from me" (DEATH, p. 228). Yet he takes charge of Jongkind, an idiot incapable even of feeding himself. Eventually Ferdinand assumes full responsibility for Jongkind and cares for him day and night. He actually worries about Jongkind's well-being: "I'm in a panic again ... I don't know exactly why. I start thinking about the kid again ..." (DEATH, p. 269). GUIGNOL'S BAND depicts Ferdinand at his nadir: selfish, hedonistic, and criminally involved. Yet during one of the many chaotic brawls that occur at Van Claben's pawnshop, he is primarily interested in saving a customer's life:

> The client in front of the counter yelps ... she's bleating with horror ... she wants to run away ... she can't! ... Everything falls all over her! ...
>
> I want the lady at least to be saved! ... My presence of mind! ... I grab hold of her again in the pile of crockery ... I pull her out again by her skirt ... (GUIGNOL, pp. 131, 133)

When the convivial Boro traps Delphine and Ferdinand in the cellar and subsequently detonates an explosive, Ferdinand once again affects a rescue: "I catch hold of her ... I clutch her by the shoes! ... I disentangle her ... I yank at her! ..." (GUIGNOL, p. 195). Much later, at the outset of the Henrouille affair, Ferdinand refuses, even for a thousand francs, to sign a certificate of madness that would put the old woman in the asylum. In fact, he is always impecunious because he charges little and is generous with his skills, serving those who otherwise might be forced to do without medical attention. For all his pessimistic moaning Ferdinand infrequently manifests an insidious form of optimism:

> I was actually finding myself much more keen on preventing Bébert from dying than I should have been on saving an adult. One never minds very much if an adult goes; that's always one sod less in the world, one thinks to oneself, whereas in the case of a child, the thing's not quite so certain. There's always the future, there's some chance ... (JOURNEY, p. 281)

Yet he hesitates to actualize or articulate his benevolence. As Céline notes the story of Semmelweiss "demonstrates for us the danger of too much goodwill toward men. (Semmelweiss, discoverer of the cause of puerperal fever, was ignored by jealous colleagues and eventually committed suicide).[15] The negative aspects of existence in Céline's world are easily discernable, but Ferdinand's positive responses toward suffering, the sick, children, and especially animals are easily overlooked.

Céline's pessimism is grounded in a grotesque comic vision of the human condition: "My _danse_ _macabre_ pleases me, like an immense farce [....] Believe me, the world is funny, death is funny; that's why my books are funny, and why fundamentally, I am full of joy."[16] The comedy provides a certain amount of relief from what at first appears to be an inexorably morbid depiction of humanity. It is the comic, in fact, that makes life bearable in Céline's world. In achieving his effect, Céline employs a varied array of techniques--satire, caricature, farce, slapstick, black humor, and so on--but regardless of the technique, his comedy always derives from extreme exaggeration. The expected and the natural are so ludicrously distorted that the comic aspect of Céline's _Weltanschauung_ must be discussed in terms of the grotesque. Indeed, although his descriptions of characters and situations are usually comic in intent, some cases are so exacerbated that they transcend the comic realm.

Céline's eccentrics fall into three categories: they are physical, moral, or emotional cripples, buffoons, and lunatics. The last group is by far the most significant. Beckett's Murphy and even West's Miss Lonelyhearts pale in comparison with Céline's gallery of lunatics: Oriental pashas, Tibetan esoterics, scratching colonialists, mad inventors--an inconceivable lot.

The truly grotesque, "the suggestively monstrous" as Santayana puts it, must be rooted in reality. The distortion of reality derives from a sudden incongruity, or "estrangement," with the actual, normal, or accepted. If the distortion derives from an a priori involvement in the supernatural, gothic, or fantastic, the result is a tale of terror or fantasy, not the grotesque. E. T. A. Hoffman, for example, creates a world of fantasy that is bizarre at times but never grotesque. On the other hand,

Ghelderode's vision and Hitchcock's PSYCHO are based on sudden distortions of, rather than breaks with, reality. They are grotesque in conception. Céline is a master of such realistic estrangement. He can be hyperbolic in the extreme, minutely revolting, and ludicrously rhetorical without transcending the realm of "possiblity." This is true even of the multitude of hallucinations that Ferdinand experiences. These deliriums, frequently caused by recurring bouts with malerial fever, remain rooted in reality instead of dissolving into pure fantasy, which would dissipate the power of the grotesque. Consequently, the gigantic Charon, who uses an oar as large as the mast of a ship to bash in the heads of the dead, is far less effective, far less grotesque in the purest sense of the term, than the malevolent Aisha, who stomps through Siegmaringen, complete with boots, whip, and mastiffs, shipping the miserable and suffering to death camps (CASTLE, passim). Céline's grotesque comedy is all the more powerful because of his use of romantic irony. When least expected, à la Heine, Céline deflates or demolishes his characters. Yet such an ultimate destruction cannot negate the comic panorama that precedes it, because, as Langer observes, "the rhythm of comedy is the basic rhythm of life."[17] The basis of Céline's vision, beneath the sordid exterior, is a devastating comedy that can release a simultaneous flow of tears and laughter.

The distorted beings whom Ferdinand meets are both pathetic and comic. Jongkind's idiocy is sad; his abandonment by his parents is lamentable; it is deplorable that he is maligned and mistreated. Yet as the butt of the other children, as their scapegoat, he assumes a comic aspect, which is understandable, because, as Al Capp said, "All comedy is based on man's delight in man's inhumanity to man." A description of Jongkind's eating habits is therefore comic in tone, though unpleasant in its

implication:

> A little screwball like that was a real nuisance, especially at mealtime, he'd swallow everything on the table, the spoons, the napkin rings, the pepper, the oil and vinegar bottles, even the knives ... Swallowing things was his passion ... He always had his mouth all dilated, distended, like a boa constrictor, he'd suck up all sorts of little objects off the floor, grunting and slobbering the whole time. (DEATH, p. 22I)

Similarly, the heinously sadistic maltreatment of Jongkind has comic

overtones because of the sexual allusions as well as his subsequent

frustrating actions.

> ...Jongkind was to blame ... the fool things he did, he was always responsible for the penalties we got ... he got his punishment ... it was epic ... They lifted up the grating and spilled him out of his crib...First they spread him out on the floor like a crab, ten of them all together gave him a mean whipping with belts ... even with buckles...When he yelled too loud, they'd pin him under a mattress and everybody stamped on him ... Then they went after his pecker ... to teach him how to behave ... till there wasn't any more ... not a single drop.

> But he was incorrigible, you'd have had to tie him to make him keep still ...You had to keep him away from the goal... The minute he saw the ball go in, he went off his rocker, he dashed in like a madman, jumped on the ball, wrenched it away from the goalkeeper... Before we could stop him, he'd run away with it ... At times like that he was really out of his mind ... He ran faster than anybody else .... "Hurray, hurray, hurray!" he'd keep shouting all the way down the hill. It wasn't easy to catch him. He'd run all the way to town. Often we'd catch him in a shop ... kicking the ball into shop windows, smashing signs... He was a demon athlete. He had funny ideas, you never knew what he was going to do next. (DEATH, pp. 232, 232-33)

Although Robinson suffers from a physiological defect, it is his ethical

distortion that is of primary concern. "Robinson survives by spitting on

morality" notes Hayman; he "does precisely what Ferdinand refuses to

do."[18] As Ferdinand's alter ego Robinson is consistently guilty of asocial

and immoral behavior. At his earliest appearance in JOURNEY he tells of

taunting a dying captain: "'Mother, mother!' he whimpered and he was pissing blood. 'Stop that!' I said to him; 'Mother! What the hell!'" (JOURNEY, pp. 38-39). Until he himself expires, Robinson manifests a total disregard for social conventions, simple appreciation, and moral standards. Ethical distortions are primary characteristics of the people who inhabit Céline's world, and Robinson is a most egregious example of such phenomena. His tenacious perversity is evident throughout the Henrouille incident, for example. Since Ferdinand refuses to send the old woman to the madhouse, her daughter-in-law convinces Robinson to devise an explosive mechanism that will destroy her. Robinson's subsequent self-induced blindness results in an agreement between the murderer and his intended victim. He shows his gratitude by once again attempting to dispatch her. This time he succeeds. During his ordeal he becomes dependent upon Madelon, a young girl who demands only love in return for her sacrifices. He adamantly refuses and ultimately drives her to distraction: "I've no longer any wish to be loved ... I hate the thought of it" (JOURNEY, p. 496). He casts off the people whom he has used with the same nonchalence that one would manifest in abandoning an old suit. His metaphysical problems are of no concern to Madelon, who is incapable of comprehending his disgust with the universe. The upshot of the affair is that Madelon kills him; Robinson's egotism precludes any other end. It hardly seems credible, however, to imply as Ostrovsky does that Robinson is actually seeking total negation and therefore incites Madelon to destroy him. Much of Ostrovsky's acclaim seems to be misplaced: "Robinson continues to be a grandiose figure, an awe-inspiring spectacle."[19] Robinson is compassionless, selfish, and unscrupulous; unlike Ferdinand, he is directly responsible for the perpetration of evil. To credit him with "heroic" proprotions or "dignity" is ludicrous.

More complex than mere physiological or ethical distortion in Céline is the malformation of a character's entire personality. If the eccentricity is limited, if the character is not literally mad, then he may be a buffoon, a creature whose antics produce unsympathetic laughter because he is the butt of the comedy, a comic scapegoat. Céline's madmen and lunatics are uproariously comic, but his buffoons stand apart because they "control" reality. The madmen are controlled by their limitations. Céline's finest buffoon is Roger-Martin Courtial des Pereires, scientist and charlatan, educator and con man, inventor and rogue. His conquests, exploits, and failures occupy much of Ferdinand's adolescence and obviously play a seminal role in Ferdinand's subsequent development. As a comic figure Courtial, of course, becomes a caricature because Céline invariably exaggerates character as well as situation.

Langer's description of the archetypical buffoon suits Courtial perfectly. The buffoon is

> ...the indomitable living creature fending for itself, tumbling and stumbling ... from one situation into another, getting into scrape after scrape and getting out again with or without a thrashing. He is the personified *élan* _vital_; his chance adventures and misadventures, without much plot, though often with bizarre complications, his absurd expectations and disappointments, in fact his whole life, coping with a world that is forever taking new uncalculated turns, frustrating, but exciting. He is neither a good man nor a bad one, but is genuinely amoral,--now triumphant, now worsted and rueful, but in his ruefulness and dismay he is funny, because his energy is really unimpaired and each failure prepares the situation for a new fantastic move.[20]

Courtial cannot be discouraged. A project that turns out to be a cataclysmic failure simply provides the incentive to attempt a new one. These projects always appear to be scientifically sound and practical but closer scrutiny reveals that Courtial's clarifications are couched in periphrastic jargon and specious terminology that have little validity. His customers, subscribers, and protégés, however, never dare to refute him.

He is too imposingly grotesque, too cocksure of himself:

> ...Whatever was said, decided, settled ... was settled once and
> for all ... no use starting up again or he'd go purple with rage
> ... he'd tug at his collar ... he'd spray spit in all directions ...
> Incidentally he had some teeth missing, three on one side ... In
> every case his verdicts, the most tenuous, the most dubious, the
> most open to argument, became massive, galvinized, irrefutable,
> instantaneous truths ... He had only to open his mouth ...
> (DEATH, p. 326)

That from a man who dresses like an eccentric clown, is disconcerting

indeed:

> Courtial had no shirt on, only his varnished shirt front over his
> flannel vest, but the vest always went way up over his collar ...
> he took an extra large size, it formed a kind of ruff, and of
> course it was completely filthy ... In winter he wore two of them,
> one on top of the other ... In the summer, even during hot
> spells, he wore his long frock coat, his lacquered collar down a
> little lower, no socks, and he brought out his boater. (DEATH,
> p. 349)

He is the raving scientist, the great schemer, the bumbling fraud, the

inveterate gambler barely holding himself together; as his balloon is patched

and repatched but continues to fall apart at the seams, so does Courtial

slowly disintegrate. Physically he keeps trim with barbells, but

intellectually he is primarily bombast, and materially he is always down to

his last franc. At the slightest sign of trouble he repairs to his basement

for "total exhaustive meditation," which is apparently his term for sleep.

In order to raise capital, Courtial organizes various contests through

his publication, GENITRON. He incites his inventor-readers to submit

plans and models for perpetual-motion machines, knowing full well that

these characters are implacable fanatics, blithering, obsessed lunatics. Or

he elicits plans for a diving bell that will be used to salvage all of the

world's sunken treasure, a project that is instigated and financed by Father

Fleury, the maddest of Céline's psychopaths. This final contest results in the destruction of the GENITRON offices, the loss of Courtial's home, and Courtial and company's escape into the comparative "tranquility" of agricultural experimentation. After the destruction of his material possessions and the loss of his livelihood, Courtial lapses into empty rhetoric: "The events have set me free[....]Profit from what you see! observe! try to recognize grandeur when you see it, Ferdinand!" (DEATH, pp. 455, 456).

The farm that Courtial sets up, to grow outlandishly large potatoes through radiotellurism, is a dismal failure. The children whom he solicits for his "Renovated Familistery for the Creation of a New Race" are an unmitigated burden. The project is the apex of his career, and in the description of it he may be heard espousing his most ludicrous explanations. The experiment turns out "gnawed, shriveled, loathsome, and putrid" potatoes filled with "vicious, unbelievably corrosive maggots" that are a regular blight (DEATH, pp. 513, 515). Courtial attempts to clarify the problem:

It's ferrous hydrate of alumina! Make a note of that name, Ferdinand. Remember it well ... You see that meconium-like substance? ... Our land is saturated with it ... literally! ... I don't even need an analysis ... Precipitated by sulphides ... that's our main trouble ... undeniably ... look at that yellowing crust ... I'd always suspected as much! ... Those potatoes ... that's an idea! They'd make a splendid fertilizer ... Especially with the potash in them ... You see the potash? That's our salvation! Potash! Potash! It's remarkably adhesive ... They're all supercharged with it ... see how they glisten ... you observe the scales? That coating on every radicle? ... All those infinitesimal crystals? ... shimmering green? and violet? ... Do you see them clearly? ... Those, Ferdinand, my dear boy, are the transfers ... Yes! ... The transfers of hydrolysis! ... Yes, yes indeed ... neither more nor less ... conveyed by our currents ... Yes, my boy! ... Absolutely! ... The telluric signature! ... That's it all right ... Take a good look now ... open your eyes to the maximum! No clearer demonstration is possible! No need of further proof! What proof? There it is ... the best! Exactly as I foresaw! ... This is a current that nothing can stop, disseminate, or refract! But it shows ... I've got to admit that ... a slight excess of alumina ... and there's another little drawback ... but it's temporary ... very temporary!... The question of temperature! The optimum for alumina is 12.05 degrees centigrade ... Aha! Remember that, O-five ... for our purposes! You follow me? (DEATH, pp. 516-17)

That is the buffoon's last peroration. Having reached a cul-de-sac, he is forced pathetically and grotesquely to blow his brains out. It is an ironic end for the encyclopedic "scientist."

Courtial's wife, Madame des Pereires, presents an extremely comic appearance. Physically transformed because of a hysterectomy, she is coarse, boorish, and prone to temper tantrums:

Frankly, she was quite a sight ... in broad daylight ... the caked powder ... the rouge on her cheeks, her violet eyelids ... those thick moustaches, and even a suggestion of sidewhiskers ... and eyebrows even bushier than Courtial's ... dense enough for an ogre, no kidding! With all that hair on her face, she'd scare her expectant mothers out of their wits ... (DEATH, p. 411)

After Courtial's suicide she comes close to the psychosis of Céline's true lunatics:

"A placenta! ... It's a placenta! I know ... His head! ... His poor head! ... It's a placenta! ... Have you seen it, Ferdinand? ... Do you see? ... Look! ... Oh! Oh! Oh!" she screamed like her throat had been cut ...

"It's him! It's him! It's a placenta! ..." She threw another fit ... She started eating her hair ... she was bellowing so loud we couldn't hear each other in the room ... The snoopers at the window climbed up on each other's back ... She bit right into her handcuffs. She flailed around on the floor, possessed. (DEATH, pp. 535, 536)

Courtial and his wife are typical bumbling buffoons: comic, ludicrous, and grotesque, but at the same time sympathisch and pathetic. Such a masterful combination of the grotesque and the pathetic is, however, not characteristic of the multitude of deranged creatures who inhabit Céline's world. Most of his madmen are so grotesque that they never elicit the reader's commiseration, even though they may be comic as well as abhorrent. His novels are replete with such psychopaths. A limited discussion of Titus Van Claben and Father Fleury will indicate the nature of "Céline's psychosis," a malady that is characterized by distortions of reality, such as hysterics coupled with physical manhandling and an inconceivable array of delusions running the gamut from grandeur to persecution.

Van Claben, nicknamed the Horror, is by far the maddest of the creatures in GUIGNOL'S BAND, a novel glutted with lunatics, chaos, and orgiastic brawls. Van Claben wears colorful silks and a turban, carries a jewel-studded cane, and is "all made up! ... a mug like a plaster mask! ... Some job! ... even worse than Joconde! and jowls, Madame! and rolls of fat with cream! and powder! ... even lipstick!" (GUIGNOL, p. 229) He raves, howls, wheezes, chokes, hallucinates, and continually demands the "Merry Widow Waltz." Ferdinand's adventures at Van Claben's hermetically sealed pawnshop consist of a series of tantrums and asthmatic stupors. Van Claben's career ends in a chaotic orgy of hallucinations that are swiftly transformed into actuality and true horror. The finale begins with a bit of smoking:

> The Horror was getting high! ... He was inhaling more than we were ... he was jumping around in his furs ... He was more comfortable, too ... he was lying down ... it was getting him real hot... He was jumping on the bed... He was getting all passionate ... even while choking away ... He grabs hold of Delphine... He squeezes her with all his might ... he throws her down on his couch! still out of breath... He puts his tongue into her mouth ... all the way in ... he's declaring his love ... while coughing and smoking away ... It was quite an act! ... the smell was revolutionizing him! Ah! I thought he was going to croak the way he was tossing around coughing ... (GUIGNOL, pp. 168, 169)

This incites Boro, an acquaintance of Ferdinand, to stuff the Horror with his own gold coins. Then with Ferdinand's help he attempts to force him to regurgitate them:

> Ah! that's the idea! ... hoist him up again by his capes, head down! ... Up the stairway! all the way up! ... Oooh! whiss! all the steps! ... the whole flight! Oooh! whiss! and up! let her go! boy, it's hard work! ... keep at it! Ah! that does it! here he is! Let 'er go! Whang! What a crash! Whang! his big head! ... the whole floor shakes with the shock! ... not a peep out of him! ... not the least sigh! ... not an oof! ... He crashed. That's all! ... We can't leave him like that! ... We jump on his belly ... we bounce up and down on it! ... to see if he's going to puke! ... Go fuck yourself! ... Doesn't say oof! ... not the slightest hiccup... We bend down to look at his face ... we put the globe lamp right against it ... his head's split. Wow! ... a hole right between the eyes ... a crack! ... a noseful of snot dripping ... hasn't said oof! Just like that, ringing his head! ... Boro stares popeyed... It's all white ... all gooey ... all the same it's a surprise... He didn't say oof! ... hasn't puked up a coin! ... not one little sovereign! ... Ah! the mule! He's stubborn! ... (GUIGNOL, p. 180)

This grotesque comedy of the demented is concluded, as in Courtial's case, by ironic deflation and hideous death. All of Céline's characters are in a continuous state of depression, decomposition, and putrification, but this is especially true of the psychopaths, such as Van Claben, Ferdinand's father, and the horde of inventors. For Céline life is all decline, and he portrays this hyperbolically in his frenzied madmen: howling, moaning, and jactitating their way to an ineluctable death.

The paragon of psychopaths, the sickest of the madmen, is Father Fleury, the priest who finances the diving-bell contest. After Courtial's escape to the country and subsequent suicide the distracted Fleury shows up at the potato farm. Barely capable of speaking, he simply dances around as if in the grip of some awful chorea:

> It took more than that to stop him... He kept on prancing ... hopping ... skipping... He didn't pay attention... He did a big leap and then some little jumps ... he jerked backward... He jumped up on the table ... He wiggled around some more ... he

jumped down, bam! ... His cassock was all caked and armored with muck and cowflop ... (DEATH, pp. 554-55)

In order to convince the priest that Courtial is dead, Ferdinand foolishly shows him the mangled body. The result is one of the most grotesque scenes in all of literature:

He doesn't want to leave... He sniffs full in the meat ... "Hm! Hm!" He starts howling! He works himself up... He throws another fit... His whole body is shaking ... I try to cover the head up again... "That'll do! ..." But he pulls at the canvas... He's in a frenzy ... stark raving mad! ... He won't let me cover him... He sticks his finger into the wound ... He plunges both hands into the meat ... he digs into all the holes ... He tears away the soft edges... He pokes around... He gets stuck... His wrist is caught in the bones... Crack! ... He tugs... He struggles like in a trap ... Some kind of pouch bursts... The juice pours out ... it gushes all over the place ... all full of brains and blood ... splashing... He manages to get his hand out ... I get the sauce full in the face ... I can't see a thing ... I flail around ... (DEATH, p. 560)

Céline is indeed "the black magician of hilarity and rage."[21] Through hyperbole he achieves an inimitable synthesis of the repulsive and the comic.

The most successful feature of Céline's repulsive comedy is the frequent need for physical purgation. As the external chaos that Céline portrays is a physical manifestation of an inner conflict or breakdown in basic values, so are excretion and regurgitation symbols of the sullied, defiled world. Emulating Don Quixote and his faithful squire, Céline's characters disgorge vast quantities of food in various states of digestion. Certainly the orgy of regurgitation during the channel crossing defies conception:

All resistance had been abandoned. The horizon was littered with jam ... salad ... chicken ... coffee ... the whole slobgullion ... it all came up ...

Up top by the captain, the first and second class passengers were leaning over the side to puke, and it came tumbling down on us... At every wave we caught a shower with whole meals in it... We were lashed with garbage, with meat fibers... The gale blows the stuff upward ... it clings in the shrouds... Around us the sea is roaring ... the foam of battle ...

A stocky little character, a wise guy, is helping his wife to throw up in a little bucket ... he's trying to encourage her.
  "Go on, Leonie... Don't hold back ... I'm right here ... I'm holding you." All of a sudden she turns her head back into the wind... The whole stew that's been gurgling in her mouth catches me full in the face... My teeth are full of it, beans, tomatoes, ... I'd thought I had nothing left to vomit ... well, it looks like I have ... I can taste it ... it'e coming up again... Hey down there, get moving! ... It's coming! ... A whole carload is pushing against my tongue ... I'll pay her back, I'll spill my guts in her mouth ... I grope my way over to her ... The two of us are crawling ... We clutch each other ... We embrace ... we vomit on each other ... My smart father and her husband try to separate us ... They tug at us in opposite directions ... They'll never understand ... (DEATH, pp. 123, 124, 125)

Yet all such negative images have positive implications in Céline. Comedy, as Feibleman observes, is "the indirect affirmation of the ideal logical order by means of the derogation of the limited orders of actuality."[22] Céline, the "comic genius, the father of verbal slapstick,"[23] by disparaging a universe that seems to produce only evil and ugliness, intimates a subconscious desire for goodness and beauty. The integral role of comedy in his total vision is indicative of this.

The pathological characteristics of Céline's various madmen, of whom we have considered a mere sampling, are reflected in two related leitmotifs, the asylum or madness and night or death. The relationship between the two pairs is interesting. Both the asylum and night are metaphorical representations of their complements, madness and death. Both are the last refuge of the outcast, the frustrated, the defeated. While in his fiction Céline consistently presents a journey to night's end, he simultaneously, though less ostentatiously, utilizes the asylum metaphor to indicate the general state of being, as well as to provide the sanctuary so desperately needed by Ferdinand and his coevals.

The asylum is first encountered toward the conclusion of JOURNEY TO THE END OF THE NIGHT. When in Dr. Baryton's sanatorium Ferdinand discovers an escape from the tribulation of the world. While ministering to the demented, he perceives the comparative peace that these people seem to maintain, at least while in captivity. Beckett's Murphy finds himself at home as an attendant in an asylum because he, in fact, craves psychosis and death as the ultimate refuge. Similarly Ferdinand finds himself envying the inmates. "I hovered," he says, "on the dangerous outskirts of the mad" (JOURNEY, p. 426). Later he finds employment at a venereal hospital, and it is from that environment that he narrates DEATH ON THE INSTALLMENT PLAN. He is himself suffering from an attack of malaria and begins his account of his abhorrent childhood in a hallucinating delirium saying, "Madness has been hot on my trail . . . " (DEATH, p. 39). The asylum motif is epitomized in CASTLE TO CASTLE, where Ferdinand lashes out from a monomaniacal perspective at his publishers, as well as at humanity in general, manifesting innumerable indications of psychosis. Eventually he turns to an account of Siegmaringen during the Second World War. The town and its castle become a microcosmic representation of a world gone mad, an asylum for "normality." Europe's dregs--the collaborator, the refugee, the sick, the hungry--gravitate to Siegmaringen. The entire world has gone mad, not just a few of its inhabitants, and the asylum is no longer capable of relieving the pain and suffering of freedom: "When the world is all upside down and it is mad to ask why one is being assassinated, obviously it is very easy to be considered insane" (JOURNEY, p. 59). R. D. Laing alleges that insanity may be a defense mechanism to protect oneself against a deranged world. Conversely, Ferdinand demonstrates that in a mad world the sane are aberrant and therefore intolerable.

Ferdinand is obsessed with the night and its complement, death. All being tends toward darkness, and the enticing night lies at the end of every journey. For Céline, however, there can be no dawning, no new day. Night implies termination: "You delve deeper into the night at first and start to panic, but you want to know all the same, and after that you don't come out of the depths of the darkness" (JOURNEY, pp. 379-80). Finally Ferdinand discovers "Truth is a pain which will not stop. And the truth of this world is to die" (JOURNEY, p. 199). At the terminus lies death, and it matters little whether the journey is brief, as in war, or slow and insidious, as it must be for the poor, the sick, and the maligned; whether death is limited, as in the earlier novels, or ubiquitous, as in the later ones. Death is the common leveler. Of course, the horror increases in the later fiction, and Ostrovsky's point is well taken: "Death is no longer on the installment plan, but wholesale and ever present. The sewers are now running blood. And the cloaca of life have [sic] turned into the charnel houses of death."[24]

Echoing Rilke ("Und dein heiliger Einfall/ist der vertrauliche Tod"), Ferdinand seems to yearn for death while simultaneously fearing it. This fascination, this peculiar obsession, can be traced to Céline's interest in the Flemish painters, Hieronymous Bosch and Pieter Brueghel. A comparison is usually drawn between these early pictorial masters of the grotesque and Céline in terms of distorted reality. Obviously this is cogent because the sudden "estrangement" discussed above is the salient feature of these artists' work. They all depict a chaotic world enmeshed in nightmare, gloom, and horror. Yet even more germane is the leitmotif of death that winds its way through medieval art and reaches it acme in Bosch and Brueghel. Bosch's LAST JUDGMENT in Vienna and the hell panel from his GARDEN OF EARTHLY DELIGHTS in Madrid affirm the grotesqueness of death and its ugliness and cruelty that cause suffering. Bosch's dismembered bodies, his conjoining of animate and inanimate objects, his monsters, and the inordinate congestion in his paintings are like illustrations of Céline's descriptions of horror, suffering, and death. Bosch is a religious allegorist, and didacticism, of course, plays a seminal role in his work. On the other hand, Brueghel manages in a theocentric era to avoid heavy-handed didacticism. As Kayser says, "Brueghel paints the increasingly estranged world of our daily life not with the intention of teaching, warning, or arousing our compassion but solely in order to portray the inexplicable, incomprehensible, ridiculous, and horrible."[25] More persuasive than the innumerable medieval renditions of Death confronting a beautiful maiden, Brueghel's TRIUMPH OF DEATH grossly distorts physical reality; the crowded canvas reiterates contorted physiognomies, skeletons, torture, suffering, and ubiquitous death. The power derives not just from the distortions, however; even more significant is the force of numbers and the multiplicity of death's guises. Céline's obsession with death results in analogous depictions:

> Bust, echo! Bust, bomb! No mistake! It's getting worse! ...
> We're going to die mashed up! ... like bedbugs! ... choking
> sulphurations! massed in the saltpeter, ravaging combustions!
> The dunghill's raving! He's eager up there! ... He's sore about
> our trouble! The awful plane! He's sugaring us again! And
> three loopings! And hail falls! ... A frying in the atmosphere!
> The cobblestones full of bull's eyes! ... The lady who got one in
> the back hugs a sheep lying there, shuffles off with it under the
> axles, creeps and convulses ... farther off ... grimaces,
> collapses, knocked over, her arms stretched like a cross ...
> groans ... stops moving! ... (GUIGNOL, pp. 7-8)

Bosch and Brueghel are Céline's spiritual forebears.

Debrie-Panel, like Hayman, Ostrovsky, Kerouac, and others, insists on the positive attitude inherent in Céline's dismal Weltanschauung: "Sous une apparence négative les valeurs spirituelles existent dans son oeuvre. Leur négation est positive ... Cette destruction n'a d'autre fin qu'une rédemption."[26] But his further contention that death in Céline's world is a condition for redemption[27] is hardly tenable. Céline can affirm without insisting that man is "saved." Death for Céline can only be a negative redeemer (since after all it alleviates suffering). This, of course, is Schopenhauer's position: death as redemption from evil (the essence of life) and as negation of individuality is the only good.[28] Such a negative redemption is all that can be allowed to Céline. Debrie-Panel implies a positive quality to Céline's obsession with death that simply does not exist.

Pathology, in its many guises, is the basis of Céline's vision. Poverty results in physical ailments; war cripples; the ZEITGEIST causes neuroses; civilization causes psychoses; and life ends in putrification and death. The physical ailments encountered are less blatant and less offensive than their social counterparts. For that reason Jongkind is ethically preferable to Robinson, even though Robinson is a far more complex character. Most heinous and most disturbing are the psychopathological disorders that are so attractive to Céline. He is fairly complete in his coverage and includes almost all mental aberrations from simple adjustment processes to psychotic reactions and organic psychoses. With few exceptions his characters are diseased, maimed, or disturbed. A whole, authentic person is an anomaly.

This essay has not attempted to categorize and exemplify each aberrancy that occurs in Céline's fictional world. Rather it has suggested the nature of its pathology and discussed the most flagrant cases. The foregoing discussion substantiates what Ostrovsky describes as Céline's "emphasis on madness and mental aberration" and the "chaotic violence and mass dementia"[29] of his world.

3. TENNESSEE WILLIAMS: EVIL TRANSCENDED

"Everything tends towards reconciliation."

--T. S. Eliot

Like Genet and Céline, Williams paints a depressing, at times grossly distorted, picture of humanity and the universe. Williams's characters invariably are crippled; if they are not physically, emotionally, or mentally deformed, they are flagrantly antisocial--alcoholic, sexually anomalous, or simply nonconforming. Yet, when compared to the unmitigated evil purposively created by Genet and narrowly observed by Céline, Williams's world allows for various forms of respite--from inauthentic escape, both literal and metaphorical, to actual salvation. Williams's critics, especially reviewers, have faulted him for not counterbalancing sordidness and disease with antithetical virtues, such as honesty, love, or honor. They fail to acknowledge that his sordid drama almost always moves toward a final moment of reconciliation. At times that reconciliation is only partial, ambiguous, or spurious, and frequently it occurs at the expense of one of the characters through violence, dementia, or death, but nonetheless it is occasionally redemptive. Such is Artaud's "Theatre of Cruelty" or, as Alfred Kazin puts it, the "Theatre of Perversion" and it is actually surprising that Williams can be both optimistic and redemptive. Whether or not these final moments allow for organic drama, humanity is redeemed. Even among the alienated dregs of humanity on the Camino Real the spell is symbolically broken by Quixote's final statement as he and Kilroy attempt their escape: "The violets in the mountains have broken the rocks!" That is not much in comparison with the preceding spectacle, but if it is true it is enough.

All characters on Williams's stage can be understood in terms of Ricoeur's ontological progression: sin/guilt/expiation.[1] Their defilement is literally a self-alienation that reflects their isolation from other human beings. Ostracized from the human community, Williams's characters are loners and outsiders who consequently become anxious, frustrated, and ultimately mentally unbalanced. Isolation, or alienation, is the key to Williams's universe; it is the basic problem from which all other complications develop. The resulting guilt can be real, as it is in Brick (CAT), or it can be subdued and metaphorical, as it is, for example, in Shannon (IGUANA) and Chris (MILK TRAIN). More significantly, however, guilt is unconsciously dissembled by Williams's characters. Through psychological transference the physical, moral, and spiritual isolation of such characters as Mrs. Venable (SUDDENLY), Mrs. Goforth (MILKTRAIN), and Princess Kosmonopolis (BIRD) results not in guilt per se but in various ugly symptoms of its consistent repression: obduracy, a sense of infallability, and self-aggrandizement. Since a person who faces a problem is far more likely to resolve it than a person who ignores or represses it, it is hardly surprising that the expiations achieved by Williams's characters are not always positive. Yet it would be extremely unfair to the groping Mrs. Goforth to deny her the negative expiation of death. Williams's methods of atonement cannot be judged solely in theological terms. Resipiscence can indicate expiation in his plays, but a sudden break with the past, sanity, or life can do so as well. In attempting to assess Williams's achievement--the pathological made bearable--one must never lose sight of these negative expiations, because in Williams's world the ultimate, if damning, fate of one character can redeem or release another.

This is not usual in artists of the pathological. Not only is expiation inconceivable in the most blatant cases--Genet, Céline, and West--but also it is highly unusual in Flannery O'Connor, Beckett, and Pinter. The progression of a typical Williams character from sin through guilt to a piacular resolution is indicative of the playwright's achievement: the subtle transformation of the psychological case study into a highly wrought work of art. As the multiple personality comes to artistic life in Hitchcock's PSYCHO or in THE THREE FACES OF EVE, or as the mad amnesiac is so poignantly portrayed in Pirandello's HENRY IV, so do Williams's diseased characters transcend their situations. As Richard Watts notes,

> The fact is ... that Williams writes with such power, compassion and insight, with such a gift for theatrical measures and amid such flashes of brooding poetry, that his plays become lyric works of dramatic art of a high and distinguished nature.[2]

Additionally, of course, Williams is a moralist. He is not simply recording various pathological behaviors from his particular point of view as a dramatist. Rather he is consistently affirming an ethical position: man is isolated and diseased, and, although he suffers, he also endures and can even achieve salvation.

In Williams's plays pathological characteristics are manifested in various permutations and combinations, but in general physical decrepitude may be taken as an external indication of an internal breakdown that is moral, spiritual, emotional, or mental. Physical distortion is not a mandatory concomitant to the more covert forms of crippling, but, when physical illness occurs, there can be little doubt that the character's interior is also in a state of decomposition. Laura Wingfield (MENAGERIE) is an excellent example of the sensitive creatures who suffer from actual physical handicaps in Williams's plays and concomitantly manifest pathological psychological symptoms. There is a direct etiological connection between her bad leg, her inordinate shyness, and the world of glass figures into which she escapes. Yet, just as her physical handicap makes her unable to cope with the world (for example, she becomes nauseous at secretarial school and stops attending), it is also an excuse to avoid involvement; the isolation of a fantasy world is preferable to the tribulations of reality. Amanda's insistence that they dredge up some gentlemen callers results in the destruction of that tenuous refuge, the secret world inhabited by living glass animals. "Go on, I trust you with him!" says Laura as Jim takes the horse. "There--you're holding him gently! Hold him over the light, he loves the light!" (MENAGERIE, p. 269). The loss of Jim, an extreme disappointment for sensitive Laura, is stoically accepted, as is the unicorn's amputation. Despite the positive effects of Jim's amateur psychoanalysis, the experience simply reinforces Laura's negative self-evaluation. The future promises little respite. She can always use her leg as an excuse for imminent failure should another genetleman caller make an appearance.

Brick (CAT) is less sensitive and more conscious of his own motives than Laura. Both his broken ankle and his broken spirit are supported by crutches, but his use of alcohol becomes a pernicious habit, and its loss is far more intolerable than the forfeiture of his wooden crutches. Brick is isolated because of his friend's death, and he is guilt-ridden because he fears that his relationship with Skipper was homosexual, and this is difficult to admit even to himself. Worse still is the unconscious dread that he was inadvertantly responsible for Skipper's death. Isolation, fear, guilt, and self-denigration are all dissolved in alcoholic stupor. As his grotesque father, Big Daddy, points out,

Anyhow now!--we have tracked down the lie with which you're disgusted and which you are drinking to kill your disgust with, Brick. You been passing the buck. This disgust with mendacity is disgust with yourself. You!--dug the grave of your friend and kicked him in it!--before you'd face truth with him! (CAT, p. 92)

Knowing the truth, however, is no panacea for Brick. He prefers to remain intoxicated. The physical crippling reflects his total inner breakdown and his adamant refusal to face reality, his own problems as well as the abhorrent world of the plantation and Big Daddy's impending death.

Physical manifestations of pathology, sometimes take a more malignant form that ultimately results in death. Big Daddy's cancer and Sebastian's heart condition (SUDDENLY) come to mind. A primary example is Mrs. Goforth (MILK TRAIN). Alienated from the human community, guilt-ridden, and supercilious, she uses others--her four husbands, her secretary, her toadies--but remains unfulfilled. Suffering from a general malaise, she attempts to prop up her being with medication--pills, injections, transfusions, and liquor: "She eats nothing but pills: around the clock. And at night she has nightmares in spite of morphine injections" (MILK TRAIN, p. 28). Although Mrs. Goforth doggedly refuses to recognize her true condition, the entire play is a depiction of her inexorable movement toward death. This "dying monster" suffers from a plethora of physical ailments that mirror her internal moral and spiritual demise.

Although Princess Kosmonopolis (BIRD) is not moribund, she is Williams's most grotesque physical cripple. Her ailments are self-induced. As a metaphorical amnesiac she blots out her unsuccessful past to others and thus is able to forget it herself. She is hypochondriacal, hysterical, and sexually frustrated. Her first appearance establishes the atmosphere as she awakens moaning for her oxygen mask, a pink pill, and liquor. When those "prescribed" remedies fail to palliate her suffering, she turns to narcotics and sexual gratification. Her purchased love is hardly satisfying, however:

> When I say now, the answer must not be later. I have only one way to forget these things I don't want to remember and that's through the act of love-making. That's the only dependable distraction so when I say now, because I need that distraction, it has to be now, not later. (BIRD, p. 47)

In fact, none of the remedies is very effective. The Princess, like all of Williams's physical cripples, needs a moral and spiritual rebirth. Her physical maladies cannot be healed until her internal problems are resolved. With few exceptions, however, such characters in Williams are past true redemption. Only Brick and the Princess totter on the Ambiguous threshold of new and authentic possibilities. Laura returns to her partially shattered world of glass figures, while Mrs. Goforth, Bid Daddy, and Sebastian all die.

If the basic sin of the Williams character is self-sustained isolation, the primary panacea is illusion. In the most blatant cases the fantasy world becomes more real than actuality, and the character can on longer face the truth or cope with reality. In at least two cases there is a total loss of ability to function in society, and the asylum seems to be the only solution. From the primary group of fantasizers five decadent women can be culled. They are all oppressed by the past and create various illusions to relieve their inability to cope with the present. Amanda (MENAGERIE) and Blanche (STREETCAR) are haunted by their glorious pasts, which are infinitely preferable, they think, to their current sordid circumstances. Mrs. Venable (SUDDENLY) refuses to relinquish the illusion that she harbors concerning past experiences and beliefs that she is discovering to be false and horrible. Mrs. Goforth (MILK TRAIN) clings to a rather tenuous group of recollections in order to bolster her self-image while blindly denying her imminent death. Conversely, Princess Kosmonopolis (BIRD) attempts to negate her past, since it is filled with imagined failures; instead, she immerses herself in sickness and palliatives. When magically "cured," she looks toward an unlikely successful future. Illusion becomes the last refuge of these broken women, and reality, truth, worth, and possibility are perverted, twisted, and molded to fit the occasion. A more detailed discussion below of some of these decadent belles will show how they utilize illusion and the resulting deterimental effects that occur.

Amanda is the archetypical Williams heroine. she has had a hard life, one that she could never have anticipated in her pampered youth: a displaced southern aristocrat, she is forced to live in a sordid northern urban ghetto, abandoned by her husband, burdened with a crippled daughter, and dependent on a "dreaming" son. In order to resolve the disparity between the past and the present, between expectation and fulfillment, she creates a primary fantasy of past splendor and seasons it with secondary illusions concerning the fate of her children. Reality is too harsh to face on its own terms, and illusion is an excellent buffer zone. Amanda's fantasy consists, first, in continually recalling her genteel past and, secondly, in attempting to transplant some of its finer points to her dingy city apartment. The incongruity necessarily results in ludicrous situations. Her very first comment is an outburst to the family breadwinner concerning his eating habits:

> Honey, don't push your food with your fingers. If you have to push your food with something, the thing to use is a crust of bread. You must chew your food. Animals have secretions in their stomachs which enable them to digest their food without mastication, but human beings must chew their food before they swallow it down, and chew, chew. Oh, eat leisurely. Eat leisurely. A well-cooked meal has many delicate flavors that have to be held in the mouth for appreciation, not just gulped

down. Oh, chew, chew-chew! Don't you want to give your salivary glands a chance to function?

To which Tom replies:

> Mother, I haven't enjoyed one bite of my dinner because of your constant directions on how to eat it. It's you that makes me hurry through my meals with your hawklike attention to every bite I take. It's disgusting--all this discussion of animals' secretion--salivary glands--mastication! (MENAGERIE, p. 237)

She treats both Tom and Laura like young children and then foolishly expects them to act in a mature responsible fashion. They have been badgered into a gentility that really cannot be related to the alien urban ghetto. Amanda's most blatantly fatuous resuscitation of the past is her constant reference to gentlemen callers. Laura, of course, has never been called upon, and Amanda's glory is rehashed at her daughter's expense:

> Amanda:
> > Resume your seat. Resume your seat. You keep yourself fresh and pretty for the gentlemen callers.
> Laura:
> > I'm not expecting any gentlemen callers.
> Amanda:
> > Well, the nice thing about them is they come when they're least expected. Why, I remember one Sunday afternoon in Blue Mountain when your mother was a girl....
> Tom:
> > I know what's coming now!
> Laura:
> > Yes. But let her tell it.
> Tom:
> > Again?
> Laura:
> > She loves to tell it.
> Amanda:
> > I remember one Sunday afternoon in Blue Mountain when your mother was a girl she received seventeen gentlemen callers.
> > Why, sometimes there weren't chairs enough to accomodate them all, and we had to send the colored boy over to the parish house to fetch the folding chairs. (MENAGERIE, p. 238)

Tom is restless and no longer wishes to tolerate his mother's rhapsodizing, but Laura, sweet, naive, and compassionate, is willing to suffer through the recital again and again including a catalogue of all the successful men her mother might have married, their social positions, and their monetary bequests.

It is difficult to decide whether such primary illusions are ultimately more detrimental than their secondary offspring. The former allow Amanda to escape into the past and avoid present responsibilities; the latter result in immediate suffering and disappointment. Amanda involves Laura in a foolish tryst with the one person she has ever liked, absurdly presuming that this must inevitably lead to marriage. Amanda is as imperceptive in this situation as she was in enrolling her daughter in business college, for which she is particularly unsuited. Laura is ill equipped for suitors, typing lessons, or a remunerative position. Amanda persists in deluding herself, although Laura insists, "I'm just not popular like you were in Blue Mountain" (MENAGERIE, p. 239). Amanda's most deleterious illusion is her belief that Tom will remain at home, continue his boring warehouse job, and thus provide her with a weekly pay check. Tom's dreams are denigrated or rejected:

Tom:
    Man is by instinct a lover, a hunter, a figher, and none of
    these instincts are given much play at the warehouse.
Amanda:
    Don't quote instinct to me! (MENAGERIE, p. 249)

Meanwhile Tom is already on his way to the adventures he craves, through the vicarious medium of film. Ironically, it is Amanda who provides the incentive for the final break. She exonerates herself by accusing her son of selfishness: "You live in a dream; you manufacture illusions!" (MENAGERIE, p. 273). Yet Amanda heads a house of illusions and is the most culpable fantasizer.

Blanche, like Amanda, palliates the harrowing present by dredging up a questionably rewarding past. She is even more refined, more genteel, than Amanda, at least superficially--though she is occasionally willing to admit that the past does not consist solely of enchanted moments, pleasure, and happiness. She insists that she is adaptable to new circumstances even though she demands coddling and compliments. In fact, she is genuinely shocked by Stella's sordid environment--the area, the buildings, the apartment, and especially the people, who are insensitive, coarse, and at times stupid:

Blanche:
    You sit down, now, and explain this place to me! What are
    you doing in a place like this?
Stella:
    Now, Blanche--
Blanche:
    Oh, I'm not going to be hypocritical, I'm going to be
    honestly critical about it! Never, never, never in my worst
    dreams could I picture--Only Poe! Only Mr. Edgar Allan
    Poe!--could do it justice! Out there I suppose is the
    ghoul-haunted woodland of Weir! (STREETCAR, pp. 19-20)

Because Blanche has no other place to go, and especially because she is lonely and requires the companionship of her sympathetic sister, she temporarily adapts to the new and unpleasant environment. This is no easy task, considering the disparity between her gentility and Stanley's coarse and insensitive nature. Their first encounter occurs directly after Blanche has privately denigrated Stanley and Stella has retired to the bathroom to wash her tears away:

Blanche:
    What's that?
Stanley:
    Cats ... Hey, Stella!
Stella:
    Yes, Stanley.

Stanley:
Haven't fallen in, have you? I'm afraid I'll strike you as being the unrefined type. Stella's spoke of you a good deal. You were married once, weren't you?
Blanche:
Yes. When I was quite young.
Stanley:
What happened?
Blanche:
The boy--the boy died. I'm afraid I'm--going to be sick! (STREETCAR, p. 31)

It is precisely because she is such a plexus of hastily devised illusions, such a broken human being, that Blanche is in need of salvation and open to love. She is not irredeemable: "You need somebody" says Mitch, "And I need somebody, too. Could it be--you and me, Blanche?" (STREETCAR, p. 96). Yet Mitch is not ready to accept her earlier promiscuity, and this final rejection is more than she can bear. She begins to retreat into herself, groping for self-respect by fabricating about her meeting with Mitch and searching for long-forgotten Dallas millionaires. In this state she is easy prey for Stanley, who assaults her. Because she cannot face the world as it is, Blanche is destroyed. In defending her possessions, she informs Stanley of her relationship with her dead husband: "I hurt him the way that you would like to hurt me, but you can't! I'm not young and vulnerable any more" (STREETCAR, p. 42). This is the ultimate self-deception, and it costs Blanche her sanity. Her world of illusion becomes a world of madness.

In SUDDENLY LAST SUMMER, Williams presents his most disturbing case of the pernicious effects of illusion and self-deception. If THE GLASS MENAGERIE is his most subtly moving drama, SUDDENLY is the most powerful. In it pathology, evil, and horror are not limited to the progenitors and the culpable. Mrs. Venable's illusion directly and disastrously affects an innocent girl's destiny. Rather than face and accept the truth, Mrs. Venable is more than willing to sacrifice Catharine. She has spent her life in the company of her isolated, inverted, and selfish son, Sebastian. Her inflated ego derives from her belief that Sebastian was dependent only upon her companionship and remained chaste. That this, in fact, is untrue, is of no concern to her, for Mrs. Venable is fortunate enough to be able to purchase truth. Nothing is ever allowed to impinge upon the ludicrous legend that she constructs for herself:

> Mrs. Venable:
>   This sounds like vanity, Doctor, but really I was actually
>   the only one in his life that satisfied the demands he made
>   of people. Time after time my son would let people go,
>   dismiss them!--because their, their, their!--attitude toward
>   him was--
> Doctor:
>   Not pure as--
> Mrs. Venable:
>   My son, Sebastian, demanded! We were a famous couple.
>   People didn't speak of Sebastian and his mother or Mrs.
>   Venable and her son, they said "Sebastian and Violet, Violet
>   and Sebastian are staying at the Lido, they're at the Ritz in
>   Madrid. Sebastian and Violet, Violet and Sebastian have
>   taken a house at Biarritz for the season," and every
>   appearance, every time we appeared, attention was centered
>   on us!--everyone else! Eclipsed! Vanity? Ohhhh, no
>   Doctor, you can't call it that--(SUDDENLY, p. 25)

She is obviously devoid of ethical qualms and goes so far as to bribe a young doctor to perform a prefrontal lobotomy on her niece, Catharine, who is guilty of obstinately adhering to the truth. Not only does she refuse to accept Catharine's revelation or Sebastian's inversion, pederastic activities, death, and subsequent consumption by a group of young anthropophagi--an admittedly horrible story, but scientifically corroborated--but also she believes that Catharine herself is responsible for Sebastian's death. This jealous, vain old woman still refuses to release her son, even though he is dead. As Catharine observes, however, "Something had broken, that string of pearls that old mothers hold their sons by like a--sort of a--sort of-- umbilical cord, long--after..." (SUDDENLY, p. 77). Cath-arine's account is insufferable and elicits Mrs. Venable's wrath: "Lion's View! state asylum, cut this hideous story out of her brain!" (SUDDENLY, p. 93). Such an insistence on maintaining an illusion regardless of the consequences to others is a fundamental characteristic of neurotic behavior. Mrs. Venable manifests a flagrantly rigid and automatic response that fails to take the circumstances into account. Such an inability to cope with reality is, of course, psychopathological. Guilt that is displaced manifests itself as supercilious or vindictive behavior. Van Kaam asserts: "If a person attempts to create reality, he is his own standard. He need not repent his mistreatment of others, for they are simply objects in a world of his own making."[3] Thus the Doctor, Catharine's mother and brother, and Catharine herself are simply pawns to be manipulated by Mrs. Venable in her compulsive desire to defend Sebastian's reputation, which even she admits is negligible.

Of the many other characters in Williams's plays who suffer from various forms of illusion and self-deception--Laura and Tom (MENAGERIE) Serafina (TATTOO), Big Daddy and Brick (CAT), Chance (BIRD), and Shannon (IGUANA)--only Serafina and Chance require special mention. Serafina, like Mrs. Venable, reveres the memory of a departed relative above all else. She purposely decieves herself into believing that her sensual husband has been faithful to her. Aspersions are cast aside or ignored. But, unlike Amanda, Blanche, and Mrs. Venable, Serafina makes the heroic effort required to cast off an overworked deception. Estelle's apodictic statement purges her:

Don't you remember? I brought you the rose colored silk to make him a shirt. You said, "For a man?" and I said, "Yes, for a man

that's wild like a Gypsy!" But if you think I'm a liar, come here
and let me show you his rose tatooed on my chest!
(TATTOO, p. 121)

She is then capable of destroying the shrine to her husband, a gesture
symbolic of her spiritual and physical rebirth. In her subsequent sexual
encounter Alvaro must not be construed as a surrogate for her husband,
who along with his rose tattoo is now entirely forgotten.

A final instance of self-deception occurs in Williams's most sensational
drama, dubbed "a highly private neurotic fantasy" by Brustein: SWEET
BIRD OF YOUTH depicts Chance Wayne's inexorable progress toward painful
disillusionment. As Princess Kosmonopolis's toady Chance's services range
from those of a chauffeur to those of a lover, but he is really only
interested in the advantages that will accrue from the Princess's connections
and money; he wants to marry his childhood sweetheart, Heavenly, but
Boss Finley, her nasty father, objects strenuously. Naturally, all of
Chance's plans are futile: there can be no talent contest; he and Heavenly
cannot become movie stars; and they both lose their youth along the way.
Chance realizes his plight, but refuses to act; if he cannot have his
illusion, he implies that he is uninterested in the future:

Princess:
      There's no one but me to hold you back from destruction in
      this place.
Chance:
      I don't want to be held. (BIRD, p. 104)

When his fantasy of future success is destroyed, Chance consciously
chooses to face castration rather than to return to a world of falsity. He
is a borken man, but unlike the five decadent belles he is conscious of a
new and authentic perspective.

In TOTEM AND TABOO Freud observes: "It is characteristic of ...
neurosis to put a psychic reality above an actual one and to react as

seriously to thoughts as the normal person reacts only towards realities."[4] Most of the fantasizers who inhabit Williams's stage are guilty of such inverted reactions. Those who are most deeply enmeshed in their own worlds, that is, those who are most in need of rehabilitation, fail to realize the extent of their malady or the deleterious toll it is exacting.

In addition to their wholesale distortions of reality, Williams's characters evidence a multitude of other pathological characteristics, both social and clinical. Where there are no actual indications of psychopathological behavior or social aberrancy, the Weltanschauung presented in the dramas frequently must be considered pathological. As Fedder points out, even the shorter works, which are etymologically related to the mature dramas, are filled with unacceptable behavior: "His short stories and one-act plays ... read like a catalogue of sexual aberrations: prostitution, homosexuality, sadism, masochism, bestiality, masturbation, lesbianism, and the like.[5] Yet to indict Williams for presenting "an abnormal psychology rather than a comprehensive philosophy of life"[6] is somewhat unfair. Despite his pessimistic and distorted view of man, he creates a tenable ontology that is far more optimistic than Céline's because he allows for normality, rehabilitation, and redemption.

Williams depicts a sordid microcosm filled with evil, corruption, misuse of power, and greed. Gutmans (CAMINO), Finleys (BIRD), Fahrenkopfs (IGUANA) and Pollitts (CAT) seem to be ubiquitous. The sordidness is made extremely clear on the Camino Real, a Sartrean land of no exit, where human worth depends solely on monetary status, dignity is nonexistent, and Gutman controls the populance with an iron hand. The innocent and naive suffer most. Thus Kilroy, as Gutman's patsy, becomes both the universal scapegoat and the redeemer. The Camino Real is an allegorical hell of desperate, suffering humanity where all redeeming activity is prohibited. As Jacques admonishes Kilroy: "You have a spark of anarchy in your spirit and that's not to be tolerated. Nothing wild or honest is tolerated here! It has to be extinguished or used only to light up your nose for Mr. Gutman's amusement" (CAMINO, p. 57). The misuse of power and predominance of degradation lend credence to the Gypsy's appraisal: "Don't kid yourself. We're all of us guinea pigs in the laboratory of God. Humanity is just a work in progress" (CAMINO, p. 113).

The social parasite is most blatantly portrayed in Boss Finley, a politician whose power and wealth increase in proportion to the subjugation of those whom he manipulates. He is a man who makes demands: he wants to be reelected; he wants Chance out of town; he wants people to believe in his masks. As he fulfills his demands, he hurts others: "I remember" says Nonnie, "when Chance was the finest, nicest, sweetest boy in St. Cloud, and he stayed that way till you, till you--" (BIRD, p. 66). The play concludes with Chance awaiting castration at the hands of Finley's son and a group of hirelings.

By portraying corruption and antisocial behavior, Williams gives his drama the atmosphere of pathology; he paints a picture of life lived in diseased surroundings. One of Williams's finest depictions of the neurotic personality occurs in BABY DOLL, a film replete with peculiar creatures. Baby Doll Meighan is a voluptuous young girl who marries in order to appease her dying father, but her eager husband must promise to wait until her twentieth birthday to consummate the marriage. This ludicrous situation is exacerbated by Baby Doll's faults: she is naive, even childlike; foolish; vindictive; and perhaps somewhat mentally deficient. The image presented in the forty-third cut captures her being perfectly.

THE NURSERY

Enter Archie Lee.
Baby Doll is asleep in the crib. Her thumb is in her mouth.
Like a child, she's trying to hold on to her sleep. Archie
Lee just whoops and hollers. "Baby Doll! Baby Doll!," etc.
"Get up...", etc. She can hardly believe her eyes....
From downstairs the pickup's horn sounds urgently. Aunt
Rose Comfort rushes in breathlessly....
Aunt Rose:
Archie Lee, honesy....
Archie:
(Very Big Shot)
Get her up! Get her up, get her washed and dressed and
looking decent. Then bring her down. The furniture is
coming back today.... He exits. (BABY, pp. 47-48)

In several ways Baby Doll is reminiscent of the precocious Lolita, though

she is almost twenty and Nabokov's heroine is barely thirteen. They are

both emotional infants. Baby Doll, curled up in a crib with her thumb

stuck in her mouth, epitomizes decadence perfectly. She does little on her

own, excluding the excellent defense of her virginity; her decrepit aunt

even has to help her wash and dress.

Through the conversations she has with Silva, Williams clearly shows

her to be a naive creature, incapable of comprehending or formulating the

simplest sequence of logical statements without becoming flustered:

Baby Doll:
Now, Mr. Silva. Don't you go and be getting any funny
ideas.
Silva:
Ideas about what?
Baby Doll:
My husband disappearing--after supper. I can explain that.
Silva:
Can you?
Baby Doll:
Sure I can.
Silva:
Good! How do you explain it?
(He stares at her. She looks down)
What's the matter? Can't you collect your thoughts,
Mrs. Meighan?
(Pause)

Your mind's a blank on the subject?

Baby Doll:

Look here, now....

Silva:

You find it impossible to remember just what your husband
disappeared for after supper? You can't imagine what kind
of an errand he went out on, can you?

Baby Doll:

No! No! I can't!

Silva:

But when he returned--let's see--the fire had just broken
out at the Syndicate Plantation.

Baby Doll:

Mr. Vacarro, I don't have the slightest idea what you could
be driving at.

Silva:

You're a very unsatisfactory witness, Mrs. Meighan.

Baby Doll:

I never can think when people--stare straight at me.

Silva:

Okay, I'll look away then.
(Turns his back to her)
Now, does that improve your memory any?
Now, are you able to concentrate on the question?

Baby Doll:

Huh?

Silva:

No? You're not?
(Grins evilly)
Well--should we drop the subject?

Baby Doll:

I sure do wish you would!

Silva:

Sure, there's no use crying over a burnt-down gin. And
besides, like your husband says--this world is built on the
principle of tit for tat.

Baby Doll:

What do you mean?

Silva:

Nothing at all specific. Mind if I...?

Baby Doll:

What?

Silva approaches the swing where she sits.

Silva:

You want to move over a little and make some room?

Baby Doll:

(Shifts slightly)
Is that room enough for you?

Silva:

Enough for me. How about you?

Baby Doll:

Is it strong enough to support us both?

Silva:

> I hope. Let's swing a little. You seem all tense. Motion
> relaxes people. It's like a cradle. A cradle relaxes a baby.
> They call you "Baby," don't they?
> Baby Doll:
> That's sort of a pet name.
> Silva:
> Well in the swing you can relax like a cradle....
> Baby Doll:
> Not if you swing so high. It shakes me up. (BABY, pp.
> 67-69)

Of course, Baby Doll fails to realize that she is the object of a subtle but contrived seduction. Silva's actions and comments hardly elicit a rebuke: "Our conversation is certainly taking a personal turn!" she says (BABY, p. 73). Baby Doll is a person whose emotional and mental growth fails to keep pace with her physical development. Externally attractive, she remains hollow and unfulfilled until the relationship with her husband is terminated.

THE NIGHT OF THE IGUANA is a study in frustruation. Charlotte, Miss Fellowes, Hannah, Maxine, and Shannon are all faced with harrowing obstacles in attempting to live meaningful lives. In Shannon, however, Williams exactingly delineates the etiology of instability in its preliminary stages. The basic problem facing the typical Williams character is isolation--from others as well as from himself--and Shannon, the partially defrocked priest, is isolated from his God, from the people he deals with as a third-rate tourist guide, from the women he would like to love, spiritually and sexually, and from himself. This loneliness deleteriously undermines Shannon's metaphysical foundation, and he becomes frustrated. Continual frustration, of necessity, results in anxiety, and this triad--isolation, frustration, and anxiety--is the key to Shannon's unstable personality. Such anxiety, as Horney points out, is a characteristic concomitant of neurosis: "There is one essential factor common to all neuroses, and that is anxieties and the defenses built up against them."[7] Typically, those defenses consist of (1) affection, (2) submissiveness, (3) power, and (4) withdrawal.[8]

Shannon at one time or another utilizes each of those protective devices. It is, however, as fruitless for him to rave and insist that he is the tour director and therefore must be obeyed as it is for him placidly to submit to Hannah's interrogation while he is tied in the hammock. His anxiety can only be cured by alleviating his isolation. That is the role that affection ultimately plays in his admittedly sexual union with Maxine. Shannon comprehends his plight, and he implies that he did too during his previous breakdowns: "People need human contact, Maxine honey" (IGUANA, p. 22). The problem is that the type of contact Shannon has been achieving is useless, as futile as his confessional letter to the bishop. His redeeming grace is a lucid self-consciousness:

Shannon:
I'm almost out of my mind, can't you see that honey?
Charlotte:
I don't believe you don't love me.
Shannon:
Honey, it's almost impossible for anybody to believe they're not loved by someone they believe they love, but, honey, I love nobody. I'm like that, it isn't my fault.

...When you live on the fantastic level as I have lately but have got to operate on the realistic level, that's when you're spooked, that's the spook (IGUANA, pp. 53-54)

Hannah's reinforcment of his own belief is an excellent antidote for his lack of stability:

Shannon:
What is my problem, Miss Jelkes?
Hannah:
The oldest one in the world--the need to believe in something or in someone--almost anyone--almost anything ... something. (IGUANA, p. 106)

Shannon, like other Williams characters, suffers from a pathological disturbance caused by isolation, the invariable evil. The solution, if there is to be one, must be sought in authentic human communication, which can cure the most diverse maladies--from promiscuity to alcoholism or dementia.

One of the ways in which Williams consistently images forth isolated human beings derives directly from D. H. Lawrence, whose seminal influence is not easily overlooked. Both authors tend to create characters who emphasize either the sensual or the spirtual. In the works of both a balanced perspective is difficult to find, especially in Williams. Fedder, in fact contends that the short fiction of these writers is created specifically "to demonstrate the negative consequences of sensual or spiritual fragmentation."[9] Either extreme in untenable, but the creatures who emphasize sexual commitment as a form of salvation are far more wholesome than those who insist on religious or intellectual asceticism. This is also true in Lawrence and in Gide. Mariam, Paul's sensitive childhood friend in SONS AND LOVERS, is really a distorting influence on him, and it is not until Paul breaks free of her that a balanced being emerges. Far more pernicious is Alyssa's influence in Gide's STRAIT IS THE GATE. She adheres to her religious asceticism with fanatic pertinacity. Similarly, Stanley (STREETCAR) may be a lusty animal, or even a brute, but Laura (MENAGERIE) is neurotic, and Hannah (IGUANA) also prefers isolation to commitment, though she insists that that is not the case. Maggie (CAT), Serafina (TATTOO), and Shannon (IGUANA) either redeem or are themselves redeemed through sensual experience, while asceticism frequently seems actually to cause problems. A coalescence of spiritual and sensual propensities is, of course, the ideal solution, but Williams never allows that to occur. Only Serafina, Shannon, and Mitch (STREETCAR) approach that ideal, and at the conclusion of their respective dramas they are beginning long, hard personal struggles.

116

A second image that is occasionally used to indicate isolation is a character's conception of God. "The courage to be," says Tillich, "is rooted in the God who appears when God has disappeared in the anxiety of doubt."[10] Both Sebastian (SUDDENLY) and Shannon (IGUANA) perversely discover in violently destructive natural phenomena the courage to be, the courage to carry on as best they can. Sebastian molds his image of God from the annihilation of newly hatched sea turtles:

> And the sand all alive, all alive, as the hatched sea-turtles made their dash for the sea, while the birds hovered and swooped to attack and hovered and--swooped to attack! They were diving down on the hatched sea-turtles, turning them over to expose their soft undersides, tearing the undersides open and rending and eating their flesh. Sebastian guessed that possibly only a hundreth of one per cent of their number would escape to the sea....

> I can tell you without any hesitation that my son was looking for God, I mean for a clear image of him. He spent the whole blazing equatorial day in the crow's nest of the schooner watching this thing on the beach till it was too dark to see it, and when he came down the rigging he said "Well, now I've seen Him!," and he meant God.--And for several weeks after that he had a fever, he was delirious with it.--(SUDDENLY, pp. 16-17, 19)

Sebastian's God-above-God is ugly, destructive, and cruel, and consequently Williams is reprimanded for his morbid, distorted vision. Consider, however, the mother's final comment:

> He meant that God shows a savage face to people and shouts some fierce things at them, it's all we see and hear of Him. Isn't it all we ever really see and hear of Him, now?--Nobody seems to know why. (SUDDENLY, p. 20)

Is it not far more constructive to follow Sebastian to a similar fate? Hurley observes, "What [Williams's] drama proclaims is that recognition of evil, if carried to the point of a consuming obsession, may be the worst form of evil."[11] Sebastian's catastrophic end seems ineluctable, and by analogy so does his mother's. Yet God for Sebastian turns out to be both salvation

and destruction.

As a priest Shannon begins with the usual Christian conception of a

Supreme Being. But a combination of hedonistic proclivities and ubiquitous

hyposcrisy brings about a drastic change in his thinking:

> Shannon:
> Look here, I said, I shouted, I'm tired of conducting
> services in praise and worship of a senile delinquent--yeah,
> that's what I said, I shouted! All your Western theologies,
> the whole mythology of them, are based on the concept of
> God as a senile delinquent and, by God, I will not and
> cannot continue to conduct services in praise and worship of
> this, this ... this ...
>
> Hannah:
> Senile delinquent?
>
> Shannon:
> Yeah, this angry, petulant old man. I mean he's
> represented like a bad-tempered childish old, old, sick
> peevish man--I mean like the sort of old man in a nursing
> home that's putting together a jigsaw puzzle and can't put it
> together and gets furious at it and kicks over the table.
> Yes, I tell you they do that, all our theologies do it--accuse
> God of being a cruel, senile delinquent, blaming the world
> and brutally punishing all he created for his own faults in
> construction, and then, ha-ha, yeah--a thunderstorm broke
> that Sunday. (IGUANA, pp. 59-60)

Like Sebastian, Shannon's God-above-God is private, exclusive, and

unacceptable to others. He is the last refuge of the isolated, lonely misfit:

> It's going to storm tonight--a terrific electric storm. Then you
> will see the Reverend T. Lawrence Shannon's conception of God
> Almighty paying a visit to the world he created. I want to go
> back to the church and preach the gospel of God as Lightning
> and Thunder ... and also stray dogs vivisected and ... and ...
> and ... (He points out suddenly toward the sea.) That's him!
> There he is now! (He is pointing out at a blaze, a majestic
> apocalypse of gold light, shafting the sky as the sun drops into
> the Pacific.) (IGUANA, p. 61)

Unlike Sebastian's malignant creator, however, the storm God of Shannon

is only arbitrarily destructive. Although these haunted characters achieve some respite through their bizarre images of God, there is a concomitant intensification of the solitude that they so desperately need to transcend.

A general evaluation of man as an isolated being can be obtained by briefly examining two plays: CAMINO REAL and SUDDENLY LAST SUMMER. Both purport to be at best parables and at worst actual exemplifications of the contemporary world. In the foreword to CAMINO REAL, Williams alleges that he has created a valid microcosm of twentieth-century life:

> Of course, it is nothing more nor less than my conception of the time and the world that I live in, and its people are mostly archetypes of certain attitudes and qualities with those mutations that would occur if they had continued along the road to this hypothetical terminal point in it. (CAMINO, p. vi)

The people--Gutman, Jacques, Marguerite, Byron, and Killroy, among others--are indeeed at the end of the road: "All maimed creatures, deformed and mutilated" as La Madrecita points out (CAMINO, p. 150). The inhabitants of the Camino Real disclose a world gone mad, a world where individuals are autonomous and "brother," that is, the attempt to negate isolation, is the ultimate blasphemy. Similarly Catharine's defense of the truth (SUDDENLY) results in an objectionable Weltanschauung:

> But Mother, I DIDN'T invent it. I know it's a hideous story but it's a true story of our time and the world we live in and what did truly happen to Cousin Sebastian in Cabeza de Lobo. (SUDDENLY, p. 47)

Critic and reader alike are hard pressed to accept that vision of reality. Falk, for example, protests, perhaps a bit too severely:

> Williams has carried his private symbolism to incredible extremes when he would make a decadent artist and aging homosexual, a sybarite who never took a stand for either right or wrong, whose sexual perversion extended to younger and younger boys, and who was finally devoured by these starving waifs--when he would

make that particular figure in the particular situation described a
symbol to represent all men of our times.[12]

Williams's world of corruption and sickness, devoid of normal people, is
aptly summarized in his poem "Carrousel Tune":

Turn again, turn again, turn once again;
The freaks of the cosmic circus are men.

Although that view is interminably verified throughout Williams's opus, he is
also capable of lyrical affirmation, as in "A Separate Poem," where "The
day turns holy as though a god moved through it." For a surprising
number of his cosmic freaks the day does indeed turn holy.

In discussing the distinction between the literature of happiness and
the literature of salvation, Charles Moeller points out that the former
portrays the embellishment and improvement of life in a world where the
possibility of being human is never questioned, while the latter is filled
with relentless threats to one's being, which force man to consider the fact
that in a hellish world being human may no longer be feasible.[13] To
require salvation, man must be in an a priori state of disgrace, or, as
Moeller puts it, "The literature of salvation is marked by the anguish of not
being able to live a human life."[14] As is made patently clear above,
Williams's world is replete with creatures in need of redemption. From that
perspective, accusing Williams of morbidity is like reproaching a theologian
for concerning himself with sin. The problem of morbidity arises only if
the playwright or theologian does not transcend the material. Williams is
often accused of having failed in that repsect, but it is the contention of
this essay that, in a subtle, and at times ambiguous or ugly fashion,
Williams's characters redeem themsleves with great frequency. No matter
how unpleasant the circumstances are, no matter how grotesque a character
appears, man for Williams has the innate potential to achieve authentic

being, for like Faulkner, Williams insists on the power of man's ability to endure: "The dominant theme in most of my writings is that the most magnificent thing in human nature is valor and endurance."[15] Endurance is thus the since qua non of redemption.

In Williams's world salvation can be achieved through the intercession of any of three catalytic agents: (1) violence or death, (2) another's sacrifice, and (3) love, in the sense of sexual union. That redemption is indeed an integral part of Williams's vision is clearly suggested by Duprey:

> Perhaps here, [in the cesspool] without straining too hard to find it, we can talk of an undisciplined, almost unconscious quest ... a longing for something half known, veiled in flesh, some breath of clear sky beyond animality and cruelty and vice.[16]

Even Mrs. Goforth (MILK TRAIN) and Sebastian (SUDDENLY) see the "clear sky," if only momentarily, through what I have called the negative expiation of death. For both of those characters death is simultaneously punishment and release from an intolerable situation. Although that may seem far-fetched, it is simply an elaboration of Williams's own theory. In the short story "Desire and the Black Masseur" he speaks of "the principle of atonment, the surrender of self to violent treatment by others with the idea of thereby clearing one's self of his guilt."[17] This is literally true of Sebastian, who presumably sacrifices himself to a violent death:

```
Catharine:
    I tried to save him, Doctor.
Doctor:
    From what?  Save him from what?
Catharine:
    Completing--a sort of!--image!--he had of himself as a sort
    of!--sacrifice to a!--terrible sort of a--
Doctor:
    --God?
Catharine:
    Yes, a--cruel one, Doctor!  (SUDDENLY, pp. 63-64)
```

If the principle of atonement is hypothetical in the case of Sebastian, Chance (BIRD) is an excellent example of consciously executed self-sacrifice. His need to expiate himself results in salvation through violence, for which he has ample historical precedent. As Tischler notes, concerning the self-destructive Williams romantic: "his destruction, for all of its seeming horror, is the only possible salvation."[18]

The second form of salvation is more readily comprehensible, though to redeem oneself at the expense of another human being may at first appear to be a spurious method of redemption. If one accepts that Williams is not aiming at a theological redemption but rather a simpler sensual and spiritual rebirth, then Tom's release from his mother's dominance (MENAGERIE) and Stella and Stanley's liberation from Blanche (STREETCAR)--both of which are achieved at great expense to other parties--can be viewed as salvations. It is true that Tom is haunted by Laura, and that the Kowalskis remain one-dimensional, hedonistic creatures, but it is equally true that they all achieve a certain degree of equilibrium, a respite from their neurotically centered pasts.

Salvation is most clearly achieved through the third catalytic agent. Love for Williams is sexual union, but that does not mean that there is no respect present. The union is not Genet's vulgar brand of sexual gratification, for Williams's characters do not simply use each other, and he implies in at least two cases that mutual respect may ultimately develop into love of a higher sort. Jackson believes that Williams

> ... draws man as a creature in need of a mode of salvation, in
> search of a power which can transcend that vested in natural
> life. Like many orthodox Christian theologians, Williams defines
> this saving power as human love.[19]

If that is overstating the case somewhat, it is nonetheless true. THE ROSE TATTOO, BABY DOLL, CAT ON A HOT TIN ROOF (both versions), and THE NIGHT OF THE IGUANA all end with positive images of love. Serafina moves toward Alvaro, shouting "vengo, vengo amore!" (TATTOO, p. 144). "Vaccarro drops out of [the] tree and stands with arms lifted for Baby Doll" (BABY, p. 140). Margaret declares,

> Oh, you weak, beautiful people who give up with such grace. What you need is someone to take hold of you--gently, with love, and hand your life back to you, like something gold you let go of--and I can! I'm determined to do it--and nothing's more determined than a cat on a tin roof--is there? Is there, Baby?
> (She touches his cheek, gently.) (CAT, Broadway version, p. 158)

Shannon and Maxine walk down the hill together, after the Iguana is released "so that one of God's creatures could scramble home safe and free" (IGUANA, p. 126). The frequency of such positive images indicates not that Williams tacked on an occasional pleasant solution but rather that salvation of a sort is inherent in his drama from the outset. In a pathological world, however, one cannot expect redemption to be blatantly portrayed. Williams provides extremely convincing verification of this and an apt conclusion to this study:

> Every artist has a basic premise pervading his whole life, and that premise can provide the impulse to everything he creates. For me the dominating premise has been the need for understanding and tenderness and fortitude among individuals trapped by circumstance.

Notes

Preface

1. See Richard Coe, THE VISION OF JEAN GENET; Erika Ostrovsky, CÉLINE AND HIS VISION; Esther M. Jackson, THE BROKEN WORLD OF TENNESSEE WILLIAMS.

Chapter 1. Jean Genet: Evil Apotheosized

1. Lawrence S. Kubie, NEUROTIC DISTORTION OF THE CREATIVE PROCESS (Lawrence, Kansas, 1958), pp. 20-21.

2. Ibid., p. 21.

3. Karen Horney, THE NEUROTIC PERSONALITY OF OUR TIME (New York, 1937), pp. 22-23.

4. Edward Glover, FREUD OR JUNG? (New York, 1958), p. 95.

5. "Deviant behavior can be the end result of two distinctly different processes.... In one extreme form, the 'behavior is psychotic, neurotic, maladjusted, or otherwise pathological from a psychiatric point of view'. The other extreme is manifested by 'clinically normal individuals' whose deviancy is due primarily to sociological factors" (Cohen as quoted in Daniel Offer and Melvin Sabshin, NORMALITY [New York, 1966], p. 107).

6. Philip Thody, JEAN GENET: A STUDY OF HIS NOVELS AND PLAYS (London, 1968), p. 30.

7. Ibid., p. 54.

8. Henry J. Yeager, "The Uncompromising Morality of Jean Genet," THE FRENCH REVIEW 39, 1 (October, 1965): 214.

9.   Offer and Sabshin, NORMALITY, p. 45.

10.   Sigmund Freud, ON NARCISSIM (1914), in GREAT BOOKS OF THE WESTERN WORLD, ed. Robert Maynard Hutchins (Chicago, 1952) 54: 399, 406.

11.   Tom F. Driver, JEAN GENET (New York, 1966), p. 17.

12.   Freud, CIVILIZATION AND ITS DISCONTENTS (1929), op. cit., p. 768.

13.   Sigmund Freud, THREE CONTRIBUTIONS TO THE THEORY OF SEX, in THE BASIC WRITINGS OF SIGMUND FREUD, ed. A. A. Brill (New York, 1938), p. 575n.

14.   Adrian van Kaam and Kathleen Healy, THE DEMON AND THE DOVE: PERSONALITY GROWTH THROUGH LITERATURE (Louvain, 1967), p. 50.

15.   Ibid., p. 49.

16.   Ibid., p. 28.

17.   Charles I. Glicksberg, MODERN LITERATURE AND THE DEATH OF GOD (The Hague: 1966), p. 35.

18.   Friedrich Nietzsche, BEYOND GOOD AND EVIL, trans. Walter Kaufmann (New York, 1966), p. 10.

19.   Barbara Leslie Gerber, "Jean Genet: The Writer As Alchemist; Metamorphosis in Fiction and Reality," Ph.D. diss., University of Wisconsin, Madison, 1968, pp. 55-56.

20.   Jonas A. Barish, "The Veritable St. Genet," WISCONSIN STUDIES IN CONTEMPORARY LITERATURE 6, 3 (Autumn, 1965): 268.

21.   Thody, JEAN GENET, p. 27.

22.   Richard N. Coe, THE VISION OF JEAN GENET (New York, 1969), p. 6.

23.   C. E. M. Joad, GOD AND EVIL (London, 1943), p. 95.

24.   Paul Ricoeur, THE SYMBOLISM OF EVIL (Boston, 1969), p. 6.

25.   John Cruickshank, "Jean Genet: The Aesthetics of Crime," CRITICAL QUARTERLY 6, 3 (Autumn, 1964): 204.

26. van Kaam, DEMON AND THE DOVE, p. 46.

27. Coe, VISION OF JEAN GENET, p. 267.

28. Nietzsche, BEYOND GOOD AND EVIL, p. 203.

29. Horney, NEUROTIC PERSONALITY, pp. 180-81.

30. Coe, VISION OF JEAN GENET, p. 183.

31. Ibid., p. 203.

32. van Kaam, DEMON AND THE DOVE, p. 58.

33. Ibid., p. 96.

34. Ibid., p. 59.

35. Driver, JEAN GENET, P. 10.

36. Ibid., p. 8.

37. Joseph B. Furst, THE NEUROTIC: HIS INNER AND OUTER WORLDS (New York: 1954), p. 90.

38. Freud, THREE CONTRIBUTIONS TO THE THEORY OF SEX, op. cit., p. 568n.

39. Glicksberg, MODERN LITERATURE, p. 36.

40. Vasili Rozanov as quoted in Renato Poggioli, THE PHOENIX AND THE SPIDER (Cambridge, Mass., 1957), p. 162.

41. Bettina Knapp, JEAN GENET (New York, 1968), p. 37.

42. William James, THE VARIETIES OF RELIGIOUS EXPERIENCE (New York, 1958), pp. 216-17.

43. Genet in an interview, PLAYBOY (April, 1964), quoted in Knapp, JEAN GENET, p. 19.

44. E. M. Cioran as quoted in Peter Caws NEW YORK TIMES BOOK REVIEW, March 14, 1971, p. 28.

45. Ricoeur, SYMBOLISM OF EVIL, pp. 5, 8.

46. Coe, VISION OF JEAN GENET, p. 108.

47. Nietzsche, BEYOND GOOD AND EVIL, p. 220.

48. Horney, NEUROTIC PERSONALITY, pp. 260, 26, 262.

49. Ricoeur, SYMBOLISM OF EVIL, p. 149.

50. Coe, VISION OF JEAN GENET, p. 309.

51. James, VARIETIES OF RELIGIOUS EXPERIENCE, p. 37.

Chapter 2. Louis-Ferdinand Céline: Evil Observed

1. Milton Hindus, THE CRIPPLED GIANT (New York, 1950), p. 54.

2. Ibid., p. 44.

3. David Hayman, LOUIS-FERDINAND CÉLINE (New York, 1965). p. 7.

4. Radoslav A. Tsanoff, THE NATURE OF EVIL (New york, 1931), p. 362.

5. Ibid., pp. 48-49, quoting Pope Innocent III in DE CONTEMPTU MUNDI, SIVE DE MISERIA CONDITIONIS HUMANAE.

6. Karen Horney, THE NEUROTIC PERSONALITY OF OUR TIME (New York, 1937), p. 290.

7. All ellipses are Céline's, unless enclosed by brackets.

8. Tsanoff, NATURE OF EVIL, pp. 4-5.

9. Paul Tillich, THE COURAGE TO BE (New Haven, 1965), pp. 139, 140.

10. Hindus, CRIPPLED GIANT, p. 93.

11. Arthur Schopenhauer, ON THE BASIS OF MORALITY, trans. E. F. J. Payne (Indianapolis, 1965), pp. 140, 144.

12. Reinhold Niebuhr, MORAL MAN AND IMMORAL SOCIETY (New York, 1960), passim.

13. Introduction by Robert Allerton Parker to Louis-Ferdinand Céline, MEA CULPA AND THE LIFE AND WORK OF SEMMELWEISS (Boston, 1937), p. xxiii.

14. Ottah Allen Thiher, "First Person Narration in the Novels of Louis-Ferdinand Céline," Ph.D. diss., University of Wisconsin, Madison, 1968, p. 96.

15. Céline in Parker, p. 39.

16. Céline as quoted in Hayman, LOUIS-FERDINAND CÉLINE, p. 16.

17. Suzanne K. Langer, "The Great Dramatic Forms: The Comic Rhythm," in THEORIES OF COMEDY, ed. Paul Lauter (Garden City, NY, 1964), p. 522.

18. Hayman, LOUIS-FERDINAND CÉLINE, p. 23.

19. Erika Ostrovsky, CÉLINE AND HIS VISION (New York, 1967), p. 147.

20. Langer, "Great Dramatic Forms," p. 514.

21. Hayman, LOUIS-FERDINAND CÉLINE, p. 46.

22. James Feibleman, IN PRAISE OF COMEDY (New York, 1962), pp. 178-79.

23. Hayman, LOUIS-FERDINAND CÉLINE, p. 46.

24. Ostrovsky, CÉLINE AND HIS VISION, p. 79.

25. Wolfgang Kayser, THE GROTESQUE IN ART AND LITERATURE, trans. Ulrich Weisstein (Bloomington, Ind., 1963), p. 35.

26. Nicole Debrie-Panel, LOUIS-FERDINAND CÉLINE (Lyon, 1961) p. 155.

27. Ibid., pp. 173, 174.

28. Schopenhauer as paraphrased in R. M. Wenley, ASPECTS OF PESSIMISM, (Edinburgh, 1894), pp. 262-63.

29. Ostrovsky, CELINE AND HIS VISION, PP. 175, 176.

Chapter 3. Tennessee Williams: Evil Transcended

1. Paul Ricoeur, THE SYMBOLISM OF EVIL (Boston, 1969), passim.

2. Watts as quoted in Francis Donahue, THE DRAMATIC WORLD OF TENNESSEE WILLIAMS (New York, 1964), p. 210.

3. Adrian van Kaam and Kathleen Healy. THE DEMON AND THE DOVE: PERSONALITY GROWTH THROUGH LITERATURE (Louvain, 1967), p. 99.

4. Sigmund Freud, TOTEM AND TABOO, in THE BASIC WRITINGS OF SIGMUND FREUD, ed. A. A. Brill (New York, 1938), p. 929.

5. Norman J. Fedder, THE INFLUENCE OF D. H. LAWRENCE ON TENNESSEE WILLIAMS (The Hague, 1966), p. 122.

6. Ibid., p. 124.

7. Karen Horney, THE NEUROTIC PERSONALITY OF OUR TIME (New York, 1937), p. 23.

8. Ibid., p. 96.

9. Fedder, INFLUENCE OF D. H. LAWRENCE ON TENNESSEE WILLIAMS, p. 27.

10. Paul Tillich, THE COURAGE TO BE (New Haven, 1965), p. 190.

11. Paul J. Hurley, "SUDDENLY LAST SUMMER as 'Morality Play,'" MODERN DRAMA 8: 393.

12. Signi Lenea Falk, TENNESSEE WILLIAMS (New York, 1961), pp. 154-55.

13. Charles Moeller, MAN AND SALVATION IN LITERATURE, trans. Charles Underhill Quinn (Notre Dame, 1970), pp. 3, 4.

14. Ibid., p. 6.

15. Williams as quoted in Donahue, DRAMATIC WORLD OF TENNESSEE WILLIAMS, p. 211.

16. Richard A. Duprey, "Tennessee Williams' Search for Innocence," THE CATHOLIC WORLD 189: 193.

17. Williams as quoted in Benjamin Nelson, TENNESSEE WILLIAMS: THE MAN AND HIS WORK (New York, 1961). p. 190.

18. Nancy M. Tischler, TENNESSEE WILLIAMS: REBELLIOUS PURITAN (New York, 1961), p. 301.

19. Esther M. Jackson, THE BROKEN WORLD OF TENNESSEE WILLIAMS (Madison, 1966, p. 58.

Bibliography

Primary Works

Céline, Louis-Ferdinand. CASTLE TO CASTLE. Translated by Ralph Manheim. New York, 1970.

_____. DEATH ON THE INSTALLMENT PLAN. Translated by Ralph Manheim. New York, 1966.

_____. GUIGNOL'S BAND. Translated by Bernard Frechtman and Jack T. Nile. New York, 1954.

_____. JOURNEY TO THE END OF THE NIGHT. Translated by John H. P. Marks. New York, 1960.

_____. MEA CULPA AND THE LIFE AND WORK OF SEMMELWEISS. Translated by Robert Allerton Parker. Boston, 1937.

Genet, Jean. FUNERAL RITES. Translated by Bernard Frechtman. New York, 1970.

_____. MIRACLE OF THE ROSE. Translated by Bernard Frechtman. New York, 1967.

_____. OUR LADY OF THE FLOWERS. Translated by Bernard Frechtman. New York, 1964.

_____. QUERELLE OF BREST. Translated by Gregory Streatam. London, 1966.

_____. THE THIEF'S JOURNAL. Translated by Bernard Frechtman. New York, 1964.

Williams, Tennesse. BABY DOLL. New York, 1956.

_____. CAMINO REAL. New York, 1970.

_____. CAT ON A HOT TIN ROOF. New York, 1955.

_____. THE GLASS MENAGERIE. In MODERN AMERICAN DRAMAS, ed. Harlan Hatcher. New York, 1949.

_____. IN THE WINTER OF CITIES. New York, 1964.

_____. THE MILK TRAIN DOESN'T STOP HERE ANYMORE. New York, 1964.

_____. THE NIGHT OF THE IGUANA. New York, 1961.

_____. THE ROSE TATTOO. New York, 1951.

_____. SUDDENLY LAST SUMMER. New York, 1958.

_____. A STREETCAR NAMED DESIRE. New York, 1952.

_____. SWEET BIRD OF YOUTH. New York, 1959.

Secondary Sources

Barish, Jonas A. "The Veritable St. Genet." WISCONSIN STUDIES IN CONTEMPORARY LITÈRATURE 6, 3 (Autumn, 1965): 267-85.

Bataille, Georges. LA LITTÉRATURE ET LE MAL. Paris, 1957.

Caws, Peter. Review of E. M. Cioran. NEW YORK TIMES BOOK REVIEW, March 14, 1971, p. 28.

Clayborough, Arthur. THE GROTESQUE IN ENGLISH LITERATURE. Oxford, 1965.

Coe, Richard N. THE VISION OF JEAN GENET. New York, 1969.

Cruickshank, John. "Jean Genet: The Aesthetics of Crime." CRITICAL QUARTERLY 6, 3 (Autumn, 1964): 202-10.

Debrie-Panel, Nicole. LOUIS-FERDINAND CÉLINE. Lyon, 1961.

Donahue, Francis. THE DRAMATIC WORLD OF TENNESSEE WILLIAMS. New York, 1964.

Driver, Tom F. JEAN GENET. New York, 1966.

Duprey, Richard A. "Tennessee Williams' Search for Innocence." THE CATHOLIC WORLD 189: 191-194.

Falk, Signi Lenea. TENNESSEE WILLIAMS. New York, 1961.

Fedder, Norman J. THE INFLUENCE OF D. H LAWRENCE ON TENNESEE WILLIAMS. The Hague, 1966.

Feibleman, James. IN PRAISE OF COMEDY. New York, 1962.

Fersch, Peter Paul. "A Study of the Grotesque in the Plays of Michel de Ghelderode." Ph.d. dissertation, Ohio University, 1968.

Freud, Sigmund. CIVILIZATION AND ITS DISCONTENTS. In GREAT BOOKS OF THE WESTERN WORLD, ed. Robert Maynard Hutchins, 54: 767-802. Chicago, 1952.

_____. "On Narcissism." In GREAT BOOKS OF THE WESTERN WORLD, ed. Robert Maynard Hutchins, 54: 399-411. Chicago, 1952.

_____. PSYCHOPATHOLOGY OF EVERYDAY LIFE. In THE BASIC WRITINGS OF SIGMUND FREUD, ed. A. A. Brill, pp. 35-178. New York, 1938.

_____. THREE CONTRIBUTIONS TO THE THEORY OF SEX. In THE BASIC WRITINGS OF SIGMUND FREUD, ed. A. A. Brill, pp. 553-629. New York, 1938.

_____. TOTEM AND TABOO. In THE BASIC WRITINGS OF SIGMUND FREUD, ed. A. A. Brill pp. 807-930. New York, 1938.

Friedman, Maurice. TO DENY OUR NOTHINGNESS. New York, 1967.

Furst, Joseph B. THE NEUROTIC: HIS INNER AND OUTER WORLDS. New York, 1954.

Gerber, Barbara Leslie. "Jean Genet: The Writer as Alchemist; Metamorphosis in Fiction and Reality." Ph.D. dissertation, University of Wisconsin, 1968.

134

Glicksberg, Charles I. MODERN LITERATURE AND THE DEATH OF GOD. The
Hague, 1966.

Glover, Edward. FREUD OR JUNG?. New York, 1958.

Hayman, David. LOUIS-FERDINAND CÉLINE. New York, 1965.

Hindus, Milton. THE CRIPPLED GIANT. New York, 1950.

Horney, Karen. THE NEUROTIC PERSONALITY OF OUR TIME. New York,
1937.

Hurley, Paul J. "SUDDENLY LAST SUMMER as 'Morality Play.'" MODERN
DRAMA 8: 392-402.

Jackson, Esther M. THE BROKEN WORLD OF TENNESSEE WILLIAMS.
Madison, 1966.

James, William. THE VARIETIES OF RELIGIOUS EXPERIENCE. New York,
1958.

Joad, C. E. M. GOD AND EVIL. London, 1943.

Kayser, Wolfgang. THE GROTESQUE IN ART AND LITERATURE. Translated
by Ulrich Weisstein. Bloomington, Ind., 1963.

Knapp, Bettina. JEAN GENET. New York, 1968.

Kubie, Lawrence. S. NEUROTIC DISTORTION OF THE CREATIVE PROCESS.
Lawrence, Kansas, 1958.

Langer, Suzanne K. "The Great Dramatic Forms: The Comic Rhythm." In
THEORIES OF COMEDY, ed. Paul Lauter, pp. 497-522. Garden City,
N.Y., 1964.

Lewis, R. W. B. THE PICARESQUE SAINT. New York, 1959.

Luckow, Marion. DIE HOMOSEXUALITÄT IN DER LITERARISCHEN
TRADITION: STUDIEN ZU DEN ROMANEN VON JEAN GENET. Stuttgart,
1962.

McMahon, Joseph H. THE IMAGINATION OF JEAN GENET. New Haven, 1963.

Moeller, Charles. MAN AND SALVATION IN LITERATURE. Translated by Charles Underhill Quinn. Notre Dame, 1970.

Nelson, Benjamin. TENNESSEE WILLIAMS: THE MAN AND HIS WORK. New York, 1961.

Niebuhr, Reinhold. MORAL MAN AND IMMORAL SOCIETY. New York, 1960.

Nietzsche, Friedrich. BEYOND GOOD AND EVIL. Translated by Walter Kaufmann. New York, 1966.

Offer, Daniel, and Melvin Sabshin. NORMALITY. New York, 1966.

Ostrovsky, Erika. CÉLINE AND HIS VISION. New York, 1967.

Poggioli, Renato. THE PHOENIX AND THE SPIDER. Cambridge, Mass., 1957.

Ricoeur, Paul. THE SYMBOLISM OF EVIL. Boston, 1969.

Roux, Dominique de, ed. LES CAHIERS DE L'HERNE: LOUIS-FERDINAND CÉLINE. Paris, 1963.

_____. LES CAHIERS DE L'HERNE: LOUIS-FERDINAND CÉLINE. Paris, 1965.

Sartre, Jean-Paul. SAINT GENET. Translated by Bernard Frechtman. New York, 1964.

Schopenhauer, Arthur. ON THE BASIS OF MORALITY. Translated by E. F. J. Payne. Indianapolis, 1965.

Thiher, Ottah Allen. "First Person Narration in the Novels of Louis-Ferdinand Céline." Ph.D. dissertation, University of Wisconsin, 1968.

Thody, Philip. JEAN GENET: A STUDY OF HIS NOVELS AND PLAYS. London, 1968.

Tillich, Paul. THE COURAGE TO BE. New Haven, 1965.

Tischler, Nancy M. TENNESSEE WILLIAMS: REBELLIOUS PURITAN. New York, 1961.

Trisolini, Anthony. "Good-bye to Love as a Literary Theme," lecture recorded at Ohio University, April 3, 1967. In the possession of Learning Resources, Alden Library, Athens, Ohio.

Tsanoff, Radoslav A. THE NATURE OF EVIL. New York, 1931.

van Kaam, Adrian, and Kathleen Healy. THE DEMON AND THE DOVE: PERSONALITY GROWTH THROUGH LITERATURE. Louvain, 1967.

Weales, Gerald. TENNESSEE WILLIAMS. Minneapolis, 1965.

Wenley, R. M. ASPECTS OF PESSIMISM. Edinburgh, 1894.

Yeager, Henry J. "The Uncompromising Morality of Jean Genet." THE FRENCH REVIEW 39, 1 (October, 1965): 214-19.